The Gold Rush

Other Books in the History Firsthand Series:

The Gold Rush

J.D. Lloyd, *Book Editor*

Daniel Leone, *Publisher*
Bonnie Szumski, *Editorial Director*
Scott Barbour, *Managing Editor*
David M. Haugen, *Series Editor*

Greenhaven Press, Inc., San Diego, California

Every effort has been made to trace the owners of copyrighted material. The articles in this volume may have been edited for content, length, and/or reading level. The titles have been changed to enhance the editorial purpose.

Library of Congress Cataloging-in-Publication Data

The gold rush / J.D. Lloyd, book editor.
    p. cm. — (History firsthand)
    Includes bibliographical references and index.
    ISBN 0-7377-0881-6 (lib. bdg. : alk. paper) —
    ISBN 0-7377-0880-8 (pbk. : alk. paper)
    1. California—Gold discoveries—Sources. 2. Frontier and
pioneer life—California—Sources. 3. California—Social
conditions—19th century—Sources. 4. Pioneers—California—
Biography. 5. Gold miners—California—Biography.
6. California—Biography. I. Lloyd, J.D., 1959– II. Series.

F865 .G667   2002
979.4'04—dc21   2001042923
                                                      CIP

Cover photo: © Bettmann/Corbis
Dover, 93, 175
Library of Congress, 142
North Wind Picture Archives, 76, 135

Printed in the USA

Contents

Chapter 1: The Discovery

Chapter Preface

1. Stumbling upon Gold
by James Marshall
In the summer of 1847, John Sutter sent James Marshall on a quest to locate timber for Sutter's Fort.
Along the South Fork of the American River, Marshall found the perfect spot and soon began construction of a mill. During testing of the newly modified
millrace in January of 1848, Marshall made the discovery that would eventually draws scores of gold-
seekers to California.

2. An Empire Crumbles
by John Sutter
After obtaining a land grant from the Mexican authorities, John Sutter began building an empire on the
Sacramento River. In 1844 he completed his fort,
which soon served as a central trading post for Northern California. Ironically for Sutter, the discovery of
gold early in 1849 at his new mill on the American
River would eventually bring his empire crumbling
down around him.

3. A Territory Transformed
by Walter Colton
As reports of the gold discovery began to reach Monterey, provincial governor Walter Colton initially
treated the news somewhat skeptically. However, in a
series of letters sent to his relatives on the East Coast,
Colton related the incredible transformation he observed in the area during the short span of three and a
half months after the discovery was confirmed.

five. Like the others in the group, the youngest, David R. Leeper, would soon discover just how unromantic the journey westward could be.

diggings at Weber Creek on July 26, 1849. A three-day apprenticeship with local Mexican and Chilean gold hunters was all Kelly required to become proficient at panning for gold.

American River, where he sometimes extracted as much as $500 of gold per day.

Chapter 4: Daily Life in Mine Country

hand at mining. He might also find himself the butt of a cruel joke.

manner of gambling operations. Seeking amusement and diversion from the toils of prospecting, many miners succumbed to the temptation. Some miners who had struck it rich in the gold fields would lose it all at the gambling tables.

Many times weighing over a thousand pounds, the grizzly bears of California were a formidable hazard to miners wandering the wilderness in search of gold. Although the animals usually avoided contact unless threatened, a few miners suffered the misfortune of a bear attack.

Having relocated to Sacramento from New York City, Dr. Jacob Stillman found himself somewhat ill-prepared for the difficulties of frontier medicine. Writing home to his family, Dr. Stillman describes all manner of death and destruction, much of which he was forced simply to endure rather than alleviate.

Located far from civilization, mining camps usually lacked the oversight of government administration. Because sheriffs and judges were rare in these isolated enclaves, local leaders were often forced to take the law into their own hands. The resulting justice was sometimes effective, but more often brutal.

Having become somewhat of a mecca for foreign-born immigrants, Sonora was consequently more varied in its culture than its counterparts to the north. Nevertheless, it was still a frontier town and was prone to somewhat primitive amusements—like the bull and bear baiting witnessed by young Canadian William Perkins one November afternoon.

Foreword

In his preface to a book on the events leading to the Civil War, Stephen B. Oates, the historian and biographer of Abraham Lincoln, John Brown, and other noteworthy American historical figures, explained the difficulty of writing history in the traditional third-person voice of the biographer and historian. "The trouble, I realized, was the detached third-person voice," wrote Oates. "It seemed to wring all the life out of my characters and the antebellum era." Indeed, how can a historian, even one as prominent as Oates, compete with the eloquent voices of Daniel Webster, Abraham Lincoln, Harriet Beecher Stowe, Frederick Douglass, and Robert E. Lee?

Oates's comment notwithstanding, every student of history, professional and amateur alike, can name a score of excellent accounts written in the traditional third-person voice of the historian that bring to life an event or an era and the people who lived through it. In *Battle Cry of Freedom*, James M. McPherson vividly re-creates the American Civil War. Barbara Tuchman's *The Guns of August* captures in sharp detail the tensions in Europe that led to the outbreak of World War I. Taylor Branch's *Parting the Waters* provides a detailed and dramatic account of the American Civil Rights Movement. The study of history would be impossible without such guiding texts.

Nonetheless, Oates's comment makes a compelling point. Often the most convincing tellers of history are those who lived through the event, the eyewitnesses who recorded their firsthand experiences in autobiographies, speeches, memoirs, journals, and letters. The Greenhaven Press History Firsthand series presents history through the words of first-person narrators. Each text in this series captures a significant historical era or event—the American Civil War, the

Great Depression, the Holocaust, the Roaring Twenties, the 1960s, the Vietnam War. Readers will investigate these historical eras and events by examining primary-source documents, authored by chroniclers both famous and little known. The texts in the History Firsthand series comprise the celebrated and familiar words of the presidents, generals, and famous men and women of letters who recorded their impressions for posterity, as well as the statements of the ordinary people who struggled to understand the storm of events around them—the foot soldiers who fought the great battles and their loved ones back home, the men and women who waited on the breadlines, the college students who marched in protest.

The texts in this series are particularly suited to students beginning serious historical study. By examining these firsthand documents, novice historians can begin to form their own insights and conclusions about the historical era or event under investigation. To aid the student in that process, the texts in the History Firsthand series include introductions that provide an overview of the era or event, timelines, and bibliographies that point the serious student toward key historical works for further study.

The study of history commences with an examination of words—the testimony of witnesses who lived through an era or event and left for future generations the task of making sense of their accounts. The Greenhaven Press History Firsthand series invites the beginner historian to commence the process of historical investigation by focusing on the words of those individuals who made history by living through it and recording their experiences firsthand.

Introduction

The California gold rush evokes romantic notions of adventurers in search of instant wealth. The period is inextricably linked to the basic idea of the American Dream—anyone, regardless of class, could head to the mining fields and find success. Although it required a sizable investment to travel to California, the playing field was certainly leveled when the prospectors arrived. In fact, those who were skilled in the manual trades were probably better adapted to the difficult work of extracting gold than their more refined peers.

While a smattering of prospectors undoubtedly got rich during the rush, many more either failed miserably or barely broke even. Others never even got started. Nevertheless, the hoards of immigrants who flocked into California in the late 1840s and early 1850s most assuredly transformed the region from a slumbering Mexican territory into an American state teeming with citizens eager to refashion their lives in an abundant land.

Setting the Stage

When Mexico wrestled itself free of Spanish colonial rule in 1821, there were perhaps thirty-five hundred colonists populating the distant region then known as "Alta California." The Mexican government's decision to remove previously imposed Spanish trade restrictions would open the territory to rapid development. During the 1830s and 1840s, the local Mexican authorities made numerous land grants, known as "rancheros," to both Mexican and foreign immigrants, and the coastal cities soon developed into marketplaces for international trade.

Not long after entering Alta California in 1839, German immigrant John Sutter became one of the early recipients of a land grant, a tract of over forty thousand acres near the junction of the American and Sacramento Rivers. His settlement, which he dubbed "New Helvetia," quickly became an important trading post in the North-Central region of the territory. Capitalizing on the fertile soil and temperate climate of the region, Sutter would expand his interests throughout the following decade into an array of successful agricultural enterprises.

As Alta California's abundant natural resources were exploited by men like Sutter and exposed to the world through trade, the territory was soon coveted by various foreign governments, but most particularly by the neighboring United States, which desired to expand its authority to the western shores of North America. Fortuitously for the United States, the Americans and Mexicans went to war in 1846 over territorial claims in Texas. When a small band of American settlers in the Northern California community of Sonoma decided to rebel against the Mexican authority in a land dispute in June of that year, the U.S. government seized the opportunity to expand the Mexican-American war into the region. By the close of that year, what had begun as a local conflict evolved into a full-fledged U.S. occupation of the territory.

As American control of Alta California continued to solidify in 1847, business was good for John Sutter. That summer, he decided that he needed a supply of lumber to use in the expansion of his main compound, by then popularly known as "Sutter's Fort." Sutter thus dispatched his construction supervisor James Marshall to search for a site with a good stand of timber to build a sawmill. Only forty-five miles away, Marshall found the perfect spot—a heavily forested area along the South Fork of the American River known as Coloma. Marshall and his crew labored throughout the fall of 1847, and by the close of the year, construction of the mill was largely completed.

A Momentous Discovery

On January 24, 1848, a mere nine days before the treaty ending the war with Mexico would be signed, Marshall discovered gold nuggets among the debris that had collected in the end of the newly modified millrace. His discovery was not only extremely ironic, but also fateful. The vast west from Texas to Oregon was about to be ceded to the United States with the stroke of a pen. In his book *The World Rushed In*, author J.S. Holliday ponders the consequences of Marshall's find:

> His discovery on the morning of January 24, 1848, might have been made at some far earlier date by one of the Spanish explorer-looters who had found gold from Aztec to Inca cities and searched the continents for more. Or Mexican soldiers in pursuit of Indians might have uncovered the first nugget and thus have provided Mexico City the means and the will to resist Yankee expansion. Instead, California's gold remained hidden through seven decades of Spanish and Mexican rule, a historical irony and a testament to Yankee luck.[1]

As a direct result of Marshall's discovery, what had previously been an underdeveloped and remote region would now be rapidly and irreversibly altered. Holliday continues:

> Everything about California would change. In one astonishing year the place would be transformed from obscurity to world prominence, from an agricultural frontier that attracted 400 settlers in 1848 to a mining frontier that lured 90,000 impatient men in 1849; from a society of neighbors and families to one of strangers and transients; from an ox-cart economy based on hides and tallow to a complex economy based on gold mining.[2]

The change would not come easily, however. The skeptical and doubtful, both in the immediate area and across the country, would first have to be convinced of the veracity of the find.

The Word Spreads

Although Sutter and Marshall wanted to keep the discovery quiet, news of the gold find began to trickle into the countryside almost immediately. Sutter quickly lost the majority of his workers, who went prospecting for their own claims in the surrounding area. A few outsiders visited Coloma in the weeks that followed, but when these visitors took news of the discovery to San Francisco and Monterey, their stories were met with skepticism. San Francisco's two newspapers made only casual mention of the discovery in March and April.

Everything changed, however, when Sam Brannan, publisher of San Francisco's *California Star* newspaper, returned from a visit to Coloma and set out to remove any doubts about the veracity of the claims. When Brannan came ashore in San Francisco, he thrust a small bottle full of gold into the air and waved his hat with his other hand. "Gold," he cried. "Gold! Gold from the American River!"[3] In his book *Gold Dust*, writer Donald D. Jackson notes that after all the rumors of the previous weeks, "the city was like an explosive lacking only the spark of Brannan's gleaming nuggets to detonate."[4]

In the three days that followed, San Francisco's population would plummet—from approximately six hundred to around two hundred. Everyone was headed for Coloma. On May 29, Brannan's rival newspaper, the *Californian*, folded up shop. Not only were there no readers, but the newspaper's own employees were deserting. The *Californian*'s last story focused on the hysteria that swept through the city: "in 'the rush for gold,' the paper said, it is every man for himself."[5] Two weeks later, Brannan's own *California Star* faded out as well. San Francisco was all but closed down.

The First Wave

Brannan's words might well mark the conception of gold fever. The previously predominant skepticism burst like a dam into an unbridled zeal to make it to the American River. J.S. Holliday documents the dreamy feelings of one of the spellbound:

> "A frenzy seized my soul. . . . Piles of gold rose up before me . . . castles of marbles, thousands of slaves. . . . Myriads of fair virgins contending with each other for my love—were among the fancies of my fevered imagination. . . . In short, I had a very violent attack of the gold fever."[6]

The rush was largely a regional phenomenon at first. Most of the people who made money with little investment came from the local area and made their claims before the end of 1848. What historian Brian Roberts calls the "poor man's rush" included Mexicans from Sonora, a few South Americans from Chile, and some deserting soldiers from the Mexican-American war.[7] Some actually found substantial amounts of the metal. Holliday writes:

> Deposits of endless centuries awaited the lucky men of 1848. Sometimes as nuggets of five and eight ounces, often as grains the

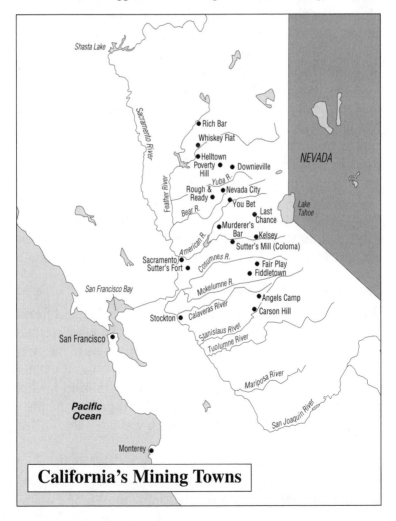

California's Mining Towns

size of pumpkin seeds, usually as flakes and granules, the gold was found . . . in myriad places—rocky bars where streams turned sharply in a canyon; widespread rock and gravel islands exposed by the low water of midsummer; narrow ravines dry after the spring runoff.[8]

Among these early prospectors were ranchers already familiar with the surrounding countryside. As Donald Jackson notes, rather than follow the herds of city folk to the American River at Coloma, "they thought of the similar streams they knew. If gold lay on the bottom and banks of the American, then why not the Feather? It looked the same, it rumbled out of the same mountains at the same elevation, it curled around low, gravelly bars and wooded outcroppings exactly as the American did. And why not the Yuba, Bear, and Consumes? Or the Mokelumne, Stanislaus, and Tuolomne?"[9] Thus the quest for gold quickly spread across a four-hundred-mile region of rivers and streams in the foothills of the Sierra Nevada.

One of the early opportunists was John Bidwell, who owned a ranchero in the upper Sacramento Valley. As Jackson records, Bidwell learned about the gold discovery while visiting Sutter's Fort on business, and after touring the diggings on the American River, "he headed for the Feather River, not far from his ranch, where his party of white men and fifty Indians cleared more than $70,000 in seven weeks."[10]

News Travels East

When military governor R.B. Mason visited the gold fields around Coloma in the late spring of 1848, he witnessed an estimated four thousand white and Indian miners in the gold fields extracting as much as thirty to fifty thousand dollars of gold per day. After his return to Monterey in June, he dispatched an officer to Washington with a report of the phenomenon. Accompanying the dispatch was a tea chest filled with samples.

It would be August before the news arrived on the East Coast. However, this and other early reports of the gold find were initially treated with skepticism by most major newspapers; a small aside printed in the *New York Sun* in October 1848 reported the gold discoveries, but somewhat skeptically included the aphorism "all is not gold that glitters."[11] The readership was likewise hesitant. In his book *American Alchemy: The California Gold Rush and Middle-Class Culture* Brian Roberts points out:

> Northeastern Americans had heard about gold rushes before, in Georgia and Alabama. To most, these western tales probably seemed little more than the stuff of juvenile fiction: believable, perhaps, to country rustics and vulgar rubes but scoffed at by more sophisticated urban readers.[12]

Philadelphian Samuel Upham summed up the early eastern sentiment:

> When the news of the discovery reached the Atlantic States . . . the early reports were of so vague a character as scarcely to be credited by the most enthusiastic, and were pronounced by the skeptical as visionary—schemes gotten up by the powers at Washington to encourage emigration to California and Oregon.[13]

Although the voices of skepticism would never completely diminish on the East Coast throughout the period of the gold rush, by the end of 1848 they would be trumped by the words of perhaps the most respected speaker in the land.

From Skeptical to Sensational

On December 5, 1848, President James Polk announced to the Congress that the gold deposits in California "would scarcely command belief were they not corroborated by authentic reports."[14] Making reference to Governor Mason's report in his address, Polk noted that the U.S. Mint in Philadelphia had received a sample of the gold, and that it was verified as genuine.

After President Polk lent credence to the gold find, eastern newspapers began to run sensational stories of the discovery. Brian Roberts notes that these publications played a critical role in promoting the rush to California:

The gold rush was a phenomenon, a ritual, not merely an event or discovery. Before the ritual could begin, a sense of "eventicity" had to be created, made appealing to a buying public, nurtured into existence by imagination.[15]

Writing for the *New York Tribune*, melodramatic journalist Horace Greeley turned up the heat on what was becoming a gold fever epidemic:

Fortune lies upon the surface of the earth as plentiful as the mud in our streets. We look for an addition within the next four years equal to at least One Thousand Million of Dollars to the gold in circulation.[16]

The great promoter Phineas T. Barnum was also prepared to capitalize on the news; he "had yellowish paint slapped on a rock, displayed it as a 'twenty-five pound lump of gold,' and positioned a real live miner (fresh from California) next to it at his American Museum on Broadway"[17] Avenue in New York City.

By the early months of 1849, eastern newspapers were filled with claims extolling the discovery. Guides were soon published explaining how to get to the Promised Land. But getting there was no cheap affair—passage alone by ship to Panama, across the isthmus, and on to San Francisco could be as high as $500, and this price did not include supplies. Brian Roberts points out that "at a time when the average American's yearly wage was between $200 and $300, the costs . . . represented something on the level of high finance."[18] Still, enough young men were sufficiently mesmerized by the lure of easy wealth that scores overcame their reluctance to abandon home and family and began to arrange for passage by sea to California. Those farther inland, being somewhat isolated from the ocean, were more likely to choose the overland route.

The Hoards Arrive

By the late summer and fall of 1849, thousands of gold seekers began to flood into California—some coming over the Sierra Nevada via the transcontinental route, others pouring in through the port of San Francisco. As Peter J. Blodgett points out in his book *Land of Golden Dreams: California in the Gold Rush Decade, 1848–1858*, "one estimate asserts that the number of miners had increased a remarkable eightfold in just a year to forty thousand. Only a year later, by the close of 1850, that figure rose two and a half times to the staggering total of one hundred thousand."[19]

The high expectations of many of these immigrants would be dashed almost immediately upon their arrival in gold country. Brian Roberts quotes the positive mood of forty-niner Henry Hyde as he arrived in San Francisco: "We expect great things, for we have a good and well-organized company." Roberts notes, however, that the optimism of Hyde's party quickly changed in the face of reality:

> A mere two days later his company voted to disband. . . . With the discovery that finding gold was a competitive business rather than the envisioned pleasure, some of the well-organized northeastern mining companies called meetings and decided that members would operate best in small groups or alone. Most simply fell apart, their members dispersing toward the foothills.[20]

The sheer competition made gold hunting at most a break-even proposition for many miners. For scores of others, the difficult work of extracting gold was enough to defeat their dreams of wealth after only a vain attempt. Having been raised in Eastern cities and far removed from manual labor, many simply could not mentally or physically bring themselves to toil through the difficult apprenticeship that would be required to whip them into shape. Most counted themselves rich men before they even established claims. Only after encountering the back-breaking labor and the high prices of equipment did the average miner consider himself lucky if he broke even.

A few of these early forty-niners did make lucrative strikes. Areas remained in the foothills that had been poorly worked by the locals, and occasionally a rich pocket of gold could still be found. But given the incredible numbers of prospectors in the region, the pickings were usually slim. Roberts points out that "promises would always overrun production. Those wishing to get a jump on the next lead or strike, or hoping to light out before the crowd got wind of it, would nearly always arrive at the next digging . . . only to find a crowd of competitors already in place."[21]

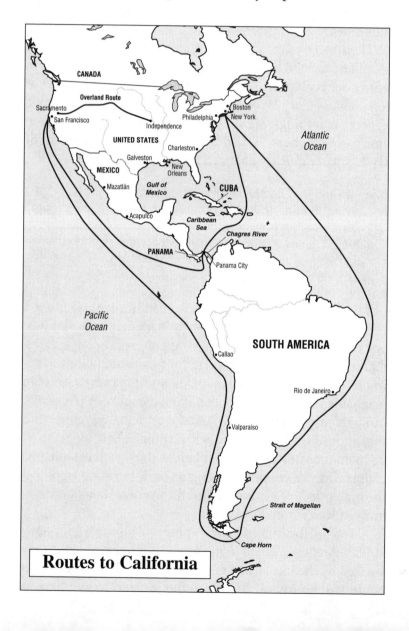

Routes to California

Although many of the early miners were failing in the diggings, the eastern newspapers continued their sensational reporting of the gold discovery. Still, the crowds kept coming.

Entrepreneurs Abound

While the forty-niners were experiencing mixed success in the gold fields, other immigrants were making different plans for enterprise in the region. Peter J. Blodgett writes:

> Before the great rush reached its second anniversary, it was clear that the wealth of El Dorado would galvanize economic enterprises of all kinds. As gold production vaulted upward from two hundred and fifty thousand dollars in 1848 to more than ten million dollars in 1849 to beyond forty million dollars in 1850 and the number of miners increased tenfold in the same period, many astute men and women saw endless opportunities from profit from the combination of vast amounts of ready money and enormous demand for nearly every commodity and service imaginable.[22]

Forced to grow quickly to accommodate the multitudes of immigrant miners, cities and small towns soon became markets in themselves, affording resourceful businessmen and women who could provide needed services the opportunity to start lucrative businesses. Some of these entrepreneurs were failed miners who had come out of the hills to resume their old occupations in the flourishing local economies.

Mining camps that sprang up adjacent to the gold digging sites also provided opportunities for enterprise. Not only mining implements were required; the burgeoning population demanded the commodities of everyday life—food, clothing, dry goods, and shelter. Saloons, gambling halls, and houses of prostitution emerged to serve the miners' entertainment needs. Laundries and boardinghouses were often overrun with customers, and professionals who could provide medical and dental services were in high demand. Prospector Mark Hopkins, writing home to his brother Moses in New York on July 30, 1850, reported that "in New York the great trouble is to find sale for goods—Here it is the reverse, our greatest trouble is in buying goods. They sell themselves."[23]

The Charm Erodes

As the miners struggled to stay one step ahead of the dwindling supply of ore and the ever increasing level of competition, the gold rush became a bust for many and a boon for a few. Long gone were the days when gold could be dug out of crevices in the rocks around creeks and streams. As Peter Blodgett explains:

> Once those [diggings] had been exhausted . . . gold hunters then faced a much more demanding prospect. To separate finer specimens of gold from dirt, gravel, and other debris, they had to find ways in which to run earth and water together, relying upon gold's unusual weight to pull the ore to the bottom of any receptacle where it would await discovery.[24]

The prospectors initially resorted to panning, which involved swirling the river-bottom debris around in a flat pan to separate gold particles from sand and small rocks. Once the digging sites were heavily worked, however, the miners were forced to construct more elaborate devices to separate the remaining small particles of gold from the dirt and sand. "Rockers," which resembled baby cradles, and "Long Toms," or extended sluice boxes, were two of the more popular contraptions employed by the miners. Blodgett points out that "miners all over the gold country adopted such advances as quickly as they could, for they found themselves in a desperate competition."[25]

While the newspapers in the east continued to report the luck of the few, the relatives and friends of the miners who wrote home began to hear a contradictory story. Brian Roberts writes:

> For many eastern observers the entire gold rush seemed like something out of the *Arabian Nights*. It contained, that is, quite a number of fascinating and gruesome tales, and much literary style, but it lacked substance. The United States Mint was reporting major shipments of gold. . . . But for wives and loved ones, the reports were nearly always the same. Their forty-niners were failing at the mines. Many had sent home daguerreotypes [early photographs]

of themselves dressed in authentic miner garb. Others had sent a morsel of yellow metal, presumably gold, enough to make a cuf-flink or a small ring. But they sent little else, apart from tear-stained letters of complaint; and they never seemed to strike it rich.[26]

A Rush No More

Before long, even the complicated gadgets devised by the miners could not extract enough gold to make the enterprise profitable. By the middle of the 1850s, only invasive tech-niques like pressurized water blasting and tunneling would yield gold, and such operations allowed a miner little more than wages working for a big employer. Peter Blodgett re-lates the travails of John Kincade, one such miner who had been left with little choice but to work for a large mining en-terprise. In a letter to his brother dated August 8, 1854, Kin-cade complained:

> All I have managed to make is a comfortable living. And that is as much as the mining population can average if not a little more. Mining is now reduced to a system. What commonly termed placer diggings being principally exhausted. The miners are seek-ing in the bowels of the mountains for primitive leads. . . . If he is not successful in finding a lead his only reward is an empty pocket and complete disgust.[27]

Sickened by the prospect of working as a laborer for a large mining operation, many prospectors began to come down from the hills. A few others stayed on, hoping that by sheer persistence they might at least earn enough money to pay for the voyage home. For these pitiful hangers-on, the gold rush, at least in terms of the prospect of easy wealth, was all but finished.

The Legacy

What is ultimately consequential about the gold rush is that people came. A few got rich, many more went home broke and ashamed, but a significant number stayed and made a life in what had become in 1850 the State of California. They populated the cities; they grazed cattle and horses;

they sowed the fertile soil. With the sea links already established from the gold rush, they formed international trading enterprises to exploit California's many other untapped natural resources.

Though the gold rush faded, the people who remained retained the hyperindividualism and entrepreneurial spirit that still characterizes American culture over 150 years after that glistening nugget caught James Marshall's eye.

Notes

1. J.S. Holliday, *The World Rushed In.* New York: Simon and Schuster, 1981, p. 25.
2. Holliday, *The World Rushed In,* p. 26.
3. Quoted in Donald D. Jackson, *Gold Dust.* New York: Alfred A. Knopf, 1980, p. 25.
4. Jackson, *Gold Dust,* p. 25.
5. Jackson, *Gold Dust,* p. 27.
6. Quoted in Holliday, *The World Rushed In,* p. 34.
7. Brian Roberts, *American Alchemy: The California Gold Rush and Middle-Class Culture.* Chapel Hill: University of North Carolina Press, 2000, p. 19.
8. Holliday, *The World Rushed In,* p. 37.
9. Jackson, *Gold Dust,* p. 30.
10. Jackson, *Gold Dust,* p. 31.
11. Quoted in Roberts, *American Alchemy,* p. 19.
12. Roberts, *American Alchemy,* p. 18.
13. Quoted in Roberts, *American Alchemy,* p. 19.
14. Quoted in Roberts, *American Alchemy,* p. 20.
15. Roberts, *American Alchemy,* p. 18.
16. Quoted in PBS's *The Gold Rush* website located at www.pbs.org/goldrush/fever.html.
17. Roberts, *American Alchemy,* p. 19.
18. Roberts, *American Alchemy,* p. 22.
19. Peter J. Blodgett, *Land of Golden Dreams: California and the Gold Rush Decade, 1848–1858.* San Marino, CA: Huntington Library Press, 1999, pp. 57–58.
20. Quoted in Roberts, *American Alchemy,* p. 156.
21. Roberts, *American Alchemy,* p. 156.

22. Blodgett, *Land of Golden Dreams,* p. 111.
23. Quoted in Blodgett, *Land of Golden Dreams,* p. 112.
24. Blodgett, *Land of Golden Dreams,* p. 56.
25. Blodgett, *Land of Golden Dreams,* p. 57.
26. Roberts, *American Alchemy,* p. 197.
27. Quoted in Blodgett, *Land of Golden Dreams,* p. 65.

Chapter 1

The Discovery

Chapter Preface

The popular history of the California gold rush usually begins with James Marshall's fateful discovery at Sutter's Mill on January 24, 1848. Although Marshall's find may have touched off the proverbial "gold rush," it was certainly not the first discovery of gold in California.

The first documented discovery of gold in California actually occurred six years earlier in the hills about thirty miles northwest of Los Angeles. On March 9, 1842, rancher Francisco Lopez, who had leased land in the area to graze his cattle, stopped for a noontime break in Live Oak Canyon. In his book *A History of California and an Extended History of Los Angeles*, author J.M. Guinn relates the events that occurred there:

> Lopez, with a companion, was out in search of some stray horses, and about midday they stopped under some trees and tied their horses out to feed, they were resting under the shade, when Lopez, with his sheath-knife, dug up some wild onions, and in the dirt discovered a piece of gold, and, searching further, found some more. He brought these to town and showed them to his friends, who at once declared there must be a placer [deposit] of gold.

Lopez and his associates began digging along the riverbanks in the area and found more deposits. Soon thereafter a small gold sample was sent to the U.S. Mint in Philadelphia, where it was determined to be of superior quality. This was to be the first gold sample received by the mint from California.

After the word of Lopez's discovery began to spread, Live Oak Canyon experienced a localized gold rush of its own. Leon Worden, a columnist for the *Signal* newspaper, reports that "hundreds of prospectors from Los Angeles and Sonora, Mexico, flocked to Live Oak Canyon, which was \

renamed Placerita Canyon. 'Placer,' of Spanish origin, means surface deposits of sand or gravel containing gold. From 1842 to 1847, the miners culled some 1,300 pounds of gold from Placerita."

Certain circumstances, however, conspired to prevent Francisco Lopez's discovery from attaining the legendary status of Marshall's. First, the placer discovered by Lopez did not have the far-reaching tendrils that those in the foothills of the Sierra did. Although prospectors from the immediate area were drawn in, there was simply not enough gold available to set off a large-scale rush. Secondly, the lack of water in the area of the Lopez discovery hampered the kind of efficient gold extraction that was achieved around the rivers and streams of the Sierra. Lastly, Lopez's find did not garner the far-reaching attention of the Marshall discovery. This resulted in part from the Placerita strike's more confined nature, but also from the Mexican control of the area in 1842. As California increasingly came under the authority of the United States leading up to the 1848 Treaty of Guadalupe Hidalgo, which transferred control permanently, the political climate became more fertile for the news of a discovery to travel eastward and for eager gold seekers to feel secure about traveling west.

Stumbling upon Gold

James Marshall

After New Jersey native James Marshall immigrated to California in 1844, he was hired by John Sutter to work as a handyman at Sutter's Fort on the Sacramento River. Interested in farming, Marshall bought a ranch in the immediate area on Butte Creek, but he continued in Sutter's employ.

Sutter was interested in expanding his settlement, but he needed lumber for new building construction. In the summer of 1847, Sutter sent Marshall on a quest to locate a timber source. Marshall did not have to travel far; only forty-five miles away along the South Fork of the American River, he found the perfect spot—a heavily forested area with good stands of trees.

After drawing up plans with Sutter, Marshall returned to the site in September and began construction of a mill. During testing of the newly modified millrace in January 1848, Marshall made the discovery that would eventually draw scores of gold seekers to California. His account was recorded in *Hutchings' California Magazine* in 1857.

Being a millwright by trade, as there was a ready cash sale for lumber, I concluded to seek a location in the mountains and erect a mill, to supply the valley with lumber. Some time in April, 1847, I visited New Helvetia, commonly known as the "Fort" where I made my resolution known to John A. Sutter, . . . and requested of him an Indian boy, to act as an interpreter to the mountain Indians in the vicinity of the American river or Rio del los Americanos, as

From "Statement of James Marshall," in *Hutchings' California Magazine*, November 1857.

it was then called. At first he refused, because he said that he had previously sent several companies, at various times and by different routes, for that purpose, all of whom reported that it was impossible to find a route for a wagon road to any locality where pine timber could be procured, and that it was the height of folly to attempt any such thing.

Seeking a Mill Site

Capt. Sutter at length, however, promised me the desired interpreter, provided I would stock some six or eight plows for him first, of which he was in immediate want, which I readily agreed to do. While I was employed upon this job there was much talk at the Fort concerning my contemplated trip to the mountains; and Messrs. Gingery, P.L. Wimmer and McLellan having resolved also to take a trip with the same object in view, came where I was working and asked me where I expected to find a road and timber, and I promptly gave them my views and directions.

They departed, I believe in company, but finally separated, and P.L. Wimmer found pine timber and a road, on what is now known as the Sacramento and Diamond Springs road and about the 12th of May Gingery and Wimmer commenced work about thirteen miles west of the (now called) Shingle Spring House.

On the 16th of May, having completed my work for Capt. Sutter, I started with an Indian boy—Treador, and W.A. Graves (who is now residing in Butte county and who had assisted me in my work and heard the conversation between Gingery, Wimmer and McLellan) accompanied me for the purpose of seeing the mountains. On the 18th of May we entered the valley of Culluma [Coloma] and . . . Gingery joined our company. We then travelled up the stream now called Weber creek—the Indian name of which is Pul-Pul-Mul—to the head of the creek; thence higher in the mountains until we arrived at the South Fork of the American river where it divides into two branches of about equal size; from whence we returned by Sly Park and Pleasant Valley to the Fort.

A Partnership Is Reached

On my arrival I gave Capt. Sutter an account of my trip, and of what I had discovered. He thereupon proposed to me a partnership; but before we were ready to commence operations, some persons who had tried in vain, to find Culluma, reported to Sutter that I "had made a false representation, for they could find no such place." To settle matters, Capt. Sutter furnished me with a Mission Indian, who was alcalde [chief administrative officer] of the Cosumnes tribe, as an interpreter and guide, trusting partly to the Indian's report, as to the propriety of the proposed partnership.

The report which I had made on my first trip having been fully confirmed by observations on the second, the co-partnership was completed, and about the 27th of August we signed the agreement to build and run a saw-mill at Culluma. On the third day (I think) afterwards, I set out, with two wagons, and was accompanied by the following persons, employed by the firm of Sutter and Marshall: P.L. Wimmer and family, James Barger, Ira Willis, Sidney Willis, Alex. Stephens, Wm. Cunce, James Brown, and Ezekiah Persons.

On our arrival in the Valley we first built the double log cabin, afterwards known as Hasting's & Co. store. About the last of September, as Capt. Sutter wanted a couple of capable men to construct a dam across the American river at the grist-mill—I sent the two Willis,' as the most capable; (Wm. Cunce being in feeble health left about the same time) and I received Henry Bigler, Israel Smith, Wm. Johnston and [a Mr.] Evans in return; and shortly afterwards I employed Charles Bennett and Wm. Scott, both carpenters. The above named individuals, with some ten Indians, constituted my whole force.

The Discovery

While we were in the habit at night of turning the water through the tail race we had dug for the purpose of widening and deepening the race, I used to go down in the morning to see what had been done by the water through the night; and about half past seven o'clock on or about the 19th of January—I am not quite certain to the day, but it was between the 18th and the 20th of that month—1848, I went down as usual, and after shutting off the water from the race I stepped into it, near the lower end, and there, upon the rock, about six inches beneath the surface of the water, I discovered the gold. I was entirely alone at the time. I picked up one or two pieces and examined them attentively; and having some general knowledge of minerals, I could not call to mind more than two which in any way resembled this—*sulphuret of iron,* very bright and brittle; and *gold,* bright, yet malleable; I then tried it between two rocks, and found that it could be beaten into a different shape, but not broken. I then collected four or five pieces and went up to Mr. Scott (who was working at the carpenters bench making the mill wheel) with the pieces in my hand and said, "I have found it."

"What is it?" inquired Scott.

"Gold," I answered.

"Oh! no," returned Scott, "that can't be."

I replied positively,—"I know it to be nothing else." Mr. Scott was the second person who saw the gold. W.J. Johnston, A. Stephens, H. Bigler, and J. Brown, who were also working in the mill yard, were then called up to see it. Peter L. Wimmer, Mrs. Jan Wimmer, C. Bennet, and J. Smith were at the house; the latter two of whom were sick; E. Persons and John Wimmer (a son of P.L. Wimmer), were out hunting oxen at the same time. About 10 o'clock the same morning, P.L. Wimmer came down from the house, and was very much surprised at the discovery, when the metal was shown him; and which he took home to show his wife, who, the next day, made some experiments upon it by boiling it in strong lye, and saleratus [a leavening agent]; and Mr. Bennet by my directions beat it very thin.

Confirming the Discovery

Four days afterward I went to the Fort for provisions, and carried with me about three ounces of gold, which Capt. Sutter and I tested with *nitric acid.* I then tried it in Sutter's presence by taking three silver dollars and balancing them by the dust in the air, then immersed both in water, and the superior weight of the gold satisfied us both of its nature and value.

About the 20th of February, 1848, Capt. Sutter came to Coloma, for the first time, to consummate an agreement we had made with this tribe of Indians in the month of September previous, to wit:—that we live with them in peace on the same land.

About the middle of April the mill commenced operation, and, after cutting a few thousand feet of lumber was abandoned; as all hands were intent upon gold digging. In December [1848], Capt. Sutter came again to Coloma, and some time in that month sold his interest in the mill to Messrs. Ragley and Winters, of which new firm I became a member. The mill was soon again in operation, and cut most of the lumber of which the town of Coloma was built.

The *first piece of gold* which I found, *weighed about fifty cents*. Mr. Wimmer, having bought a stock of merchandise some time about May or June, 1848; and Mrs. Wimmer being my treasurer, used four hundred and forty dollars of my money to complete the purchase; and among which was the first piece of gold which I had found. Where that went or where it is now, I believe that nobody knows.

An Empire Crumbles

John Sutter

> After a series of business failures in his native Germany, John
> Sutter decided to try his fortune elsewhere. Deeply in debt
> and besieged by creditors, he left his wife and four children
> behind in Europe in 1834 and made his way to America.
>
> Sutter initially resided in Missouri, but dreams of estab-
> lishing an agricultural empire in the west led him to Califor-
> nia in 1839. After gaining approval from the Mexican authori-
> ties, he settled at the forks of the American and Sacramento
> Rivers. The following year he became a Mexican citizen,
> which qualified him for the land grant of almost fifty thou-
> sand acres he would receive in 1841.
>
> Sutter christened his grant New Helvetia and began build-
> ing his empire. He soon established successful operations in
> wheat farming, cattle and horse ranching, and trapping, and
> his fort, which was completed in 1844, served as a central
> trading post for Northern California. Ironically for Sutter, the
> discovery of gold early in 1849 at his new mill on the Ameri-
> can River would eventually bring his empire crumbling down
> around him. Sutter gave his account of the rise and fall of his
> empire to *Hutchings' California Magazine* in 1857.

It was in the first part of January, 1848, when the gold was
discovered at Coloma, where I was then building a saw-
mill. The contractor and builder of this mill was James W.
Marshall, from New Jersey. In the fall of 1847, after the mill
seat had been located, I sent up to this place Mr. P.L. Wimmer with his family, and a number of laborers, from the dis-

From John Sutter, "The Discovery of Gold in California," *Hutchings' California Magazine*, November 1857.

banded Mormon Battalion; and a little later I engaged Mr. Bennet from Oregon to assist Mr. Marshall in the mechanical labors of the mill. Mr. Wimmer had the team in charge, assisted by his young sons, to do the necessary teaming, and Mrs. Wimmer did the cooking for all hands.

The First Report

I was very much in need of a new saw-mill, to get lumber to finish my large flouring mill . . . at Brighton, which was commenced at the same time, and was rapidly progressing; likewise for other buildings, fences, etc., for the small village of Yerba Buena (now San Francisco). In the City Hotel (the only one), at the dinner table this enterprise was unkindly called "another folly of Sutter's," as my first settlement at the old fort near Sacramento City was called by a good many, "a folly of his," and they were about right in that, because I had the best chances to get some of the finest locations near the settlements; and even well stocked ranchos had been offered to me on the most reasonable conditions; but I refused all these good offers, and preferred to explore the wilderness, and select a territory on the banks of the Sacramento. It was a rainy afternoon when Mr. Marshall arrived at my office in the Fort, very wet. I was somewhat surprised to see him, as he was down a few days previous; and then, I sent up to Coloma a number of teams with provisions, mill irons, etc., etc. He told me then that he had some important and interesting news which he wished to communicate secretly to me, and wished me to go with him to a place where we should not be disturbed, and where no listeners could come and hear what we had to say. I went with him to my private rooms; he requested me to lock the door; I complied, but I told him at the same time that nobody was in the house except the clerk, who was in his office in a different part of the house; after requesting of me something which he wanted, which my servants brought and then left the room, I forgot to lock the doors, and it happened that the door was opened by the clerk just at the moment when Marshall took a rag from his pocket, showing me the yellow metal: he had about two ounces of it; but how quick Mr. M. put the yellow metal in his pocket again can hardly be described. The clerk came to see me on business, and excused himself for interrupting me, and as soon as he had left I was told, "now lock the doors; didn't I tell you that we might have listeners?" I told him that he need fear nothing about that, as it was not the habit of this gentleman; but I could hardly convince him that he need not to be suspicious. Then Mr. M. began to show me this metal, which consisted of small pieces and specimens, some of them worth a few dollars; he told me that he had expressed his opinion to the laborers at the mill that this might be gold; but some of them were laughing at him and called him a crazy man, and could not believe such a thing.

Verifying the Evidence

After having proved the metal with aqua fortis [chemical used to test gold], which I found in my apothecary shop, likewise with other experiments, and read the long article "gold" in the *Encyclopedia Americana,* I declared this to be gold of the finest quality, of at least 23 carats. After this Mr. M. had no more rest nor patience, and wanted me to start with him immediately for Coloma; but I told him I could not leave as it was late in the evening and nearly supper time, and that it would be better for him to remain with me till the next morning, and I would travel with him, but this would not do: he asked me only "will you come to-morrow morning?" I told him yes, and off he started for Coloma in the heaviest rain, although already very wet, taking nothing to eat. I took this news very easy, like all other occurrences good or bad, but thought a great deal during the night about the consequences which might follow such a discovery. I gave all my necessary orders to my numerous laborers, and left the next morning at 7 o'clock, accompanied by an Indian soldier, and vaquero [cowboy], in a heavy rain, for Coloma. About half way on the road I saw at a distance a human being crawling out from the brushwood. I asked the Indian who it was: he told me "the same man who was with you last evening." When I came nearer I found it was Marshall, very wet; I told him that he would have done better to remain with me at the fort than to pass such an ugly night here but he told me that he went up to Coloma (54 miles), took his other horse and came half way to meet me; then we rode up to the new Eldorado. In the afternoon the weather was clearing up, and we made a prospecting promenade. The next morning we went to the tail-race of the mill, through which the water was running during the night, to clean out the gravel which had been made loose, for the purpose of widening the race; and after the water was out of the race we went in to search for gold. This was done every morning: small pieces of gold could be seen remaining on the bottom of the clean washed bed rock. I went in the race and picked up several pieces of this gold, several of the laborers gave me some which they had picked up, and from Marshall I received a part. I told them that I would get a ring made of this gold as soon as it could be done in California; and I have had a heavy ring made, with my family's [coat] of arms engraved on the outside, and on the inside of the ring is engraved, "The first gold, discovered in January, 1848." Now if Mrs. Wimmer possesses a piece which has been found earlier than mine Mr. Marshall can tell, as it was probably received from him. I think Mr. Marshall could have hardly known himself which was exactly the first little piece, among the whole.

An Explosive Secret

The next day I went with Mr. M. on a prospecting tour in the vicinity of Coloma, and the following morning I left for Sacramento. Before my departure I had a conversation with all hands: I told them that I would consider it as a great favor if they would keep this discovery secret only for six weeks, so that I could finish my large flour mill at Brighton, . . . which had cost me already about from 24 to 25,000 dollars—the people up there promised to keep it secret so long. On my way home, instead of feeling happy and contented, I was very unhappy, and could not see that it would benefit me much, and I was perfectly right in thinking so; as it came just precisely as I expected. I thought at the same time that it could hardly be kept secret for six weeks, and in this I was not mistaken, for about two weeks later, after my return, I sent up several teams in charge of a white man, as the teamsters were Indian boys. This man was acquainted with all hands up there, and Mrs. Wimmer told him the whole secret; likewise the young sons of Mr. Wimmer told him that they had gold, and that they would let him have some too; and so he obtained a few dollars' worth of it as a present. As soon as this man arrived at the fort he went to a small store in one of my outside buildings, kept by Mr. Smith, a partner of Samuel Brannan, and asked for a bottle of brandy, for which he would pay the cash; after having the bottle he paid with these small pieces of gold. Smith was astonished and asked

The Iconoclast

By all accounts, John Sutter was a man who followed his own drummer. Although he was often stubborn, he was also a man of vision. As historian Donald B. Chidsey points out, when searching for the right location for his "New Helvetia," Sutter ignored the cool-headed advice of his acquaintances and trusted his own instincts.

When John Augustus Sutter put in at [San Francisco] . . . Mexico still ruled upper California, more or less. Sutter, like all Swiss, was a polyglot. He was soon to add Spanish to the tongues he had mastered, including German, French, and English, and recently a smattering of Hawaiian; and if he spoke all of these with an accent it was a *charming* accent, and he was glib. He spent little time in talking the governor, Juan Bautista Alvarado, into granting him eleven square leagues—all the law allowed—roughly 50,000 acres—in the valley of the Sacramento River. This was the wildest part of the wilderness. There was nothing there but trees and rocks and streams and occasionally a wandering band of Indians. Sutter named it New Helvetia. Far inland, him if he intended to insult him; the teamster told him to go and ask me about it; Smith came in, in great haste, to see me, and I told him at once the truth—what could I do? I had to tell him all about it. He reported it to Mr. S. Brannan, who came up immediately to get all possible information, when he returned and sent up large supplies of goods, leased a larger house from me, and commenced a very large and profitable business; soon he opened a branch house of business at Mormon Island.

Mr. Brannan made a kind of claim on Mormon Island, and put a tolerably heavy tax on "The Latter Day Saints." I believe it was 30 per cent, which they paid for some time, until they got tired of it (some of them told me that it was for the purpose of building a temple for the honor and glory of the Lord).

---

it had probably never had a name before.

Everybody he conferred with—and he knew every white man of importance in northern California, for he was a great hand with a letter of introduction—advised him against going so far back into the wilderness. Settle nearer to the shore, they urged. But he was firm. He wanted, above all, to be his own boss. He did not wish to be close to the government of California, weak and amiable though that government was. So—off he went.

He settled at the junction of the American and Sacramento rivers, about 60 miles from the sea. . . .

After a year, the law had it, he could become a full Mexican citizen, and at last legal owner of the land. He had plans for new structures, the establishment of a whole city. Adobe he had, and there were plenty of logs, but the process of sawing logs into boards by hand was a long and laborious one. If only he could build a sawmill he would have all he needed and even a surplus that could be floated down the river for sale at Yerba Buena—or San Francisco, as it was being called now, the cove having been filled in.

Donald B. Chidsey, *The California Gold Rush.* New York: Crown Publishers, 1968.

The Rush Begins

So soon as the secret was out my laborers began to leave me, in small parties first, but then all left, from the clerk to the cook, and I was in great distress; only a few mechanics remained to finish some very necessary work which they had commenced, and about eight invalids, who continued slowly to work a few teams, to scrape out the mill race at Brighton. The Mormons did not like to leave my mill unfinished, but they got the gold fever like everybody else. After they had made their piles they left for the Great Salt Lake. So long as these people have been employed by me they have behaved very well, and were industrious and faithful laborers, and when settling their accounts there was not one of them who was not contented and satisfied.

Then the people commenced rushing up from San Francisco and other parts of California, in May, 1848: in the former village only five men were left to take care of the women and children. The single men locked their doors and left for "Sutter's Fort," and from there to the Eldorado. For some time the people in Monterey and farther south would not believe the news of the gold discovery, and said that it was only a 'Ruse de Guerre' [trick of war] of Sutter's, because he wanted to have neighbors in his wilderness. From this time on I got only too many neighbors, and some very bad ones among them.

Fortune Reaps Misfortune

What a great misfortune was this sudden gold discovery for me! It has just broken up and ruined my hard, restless, and industrious labors, connected with many dangers of life, as I had many narrow escapes before I became properly established.

From my mill buildings I reaped no benefit whatever, the mill stones even have been stolen and sold.

My tannery, which was then in a flourishing condition, and was carried on very profitably, was deserted, a large quantity of leather was left unfinished in the vats; and a great quantity of raw hides became valueless as they could not be sold; nobody wanted to be bothered with such trash, as it was called. So it was in all the other mechanical trades which I had carried on; all was abandoned, and work commenced or nearly finished was all left, to an immense loss for me. Even the Indians had no more patience to work alone, in harvesting and threshing my large wheat crop out; as the whites had all left, and other Indians had been engaged by some white men to work for them, and they commenced to have some gold for which they were buying all kinds of articles at enormous prices in the stores; which, when my Indians saw this, they wished very much to go to the mountains and dig gold. At last I consented, got a number of wagons ready, loaded them with provisions and goods of all kinds, employed a clerk, and left with about one hundred Indians, and about fifty Sandwich Islanders (Kanakas) which had joined those which I brought with me from the Islands. The first camp was about ten miles above Mormon Island, on the south fork of the American river.

Getting Out of the Gold Business

In a few weeks we became crowded, and it would no more pay, as my people made too many acquaintances. I broke up the camp and started on the march further south, and located my next camp on Sutter creek (now in Amador County), and thought that I should there be alone. The work was going on well for a while, until three or four traveling grog-shops surrounded me, at from one and 8, half to two miles distance from the camp; then, of course, the gold was taken to these places, for drinking, gambling, etc., and then the following day they were sick and unable to work, and became deeper and more indebted to me, and particularly the Kanakas. I found that it was high time to quit this kind of business, and lose no more time and money. I therefore broke up the camp and returned to the Fort, where I disbanded nearly all the people who had worked for me in the mountains digging gold. This whole expedition proved to be a heavy loss to me.

At the same time I was engaged in a mercantile firm in Coloma, which I left in January, 1849—likewise with many sacrifices. After this I would have nothing more to do with the gold affairs. At this time, the Fort was the great trading place where nearly all the business was transacted. I had no pleasure to remain there, and moved up to Hock Farm, with all my Indians, and who had been with me from the time they were children. The place was then in charge of a Major Domo.

It is very singular that the Indians never found a piece of gold and brought it to me, as they very often did other specimens found in the ravines. I requested them continually to bring me some curiosities from the mountains, for which I always recompensed them. I have received animals, birds, plants, young trees, wild fruits, pipe clay, stones, red ochre, etc., etc., but never a piece of gold. Mr. Dana of the scientific corps of the expedition under Com. Wilkes' Exploring Squadron, told me that he had the strongest proof and signs of gold in the vicinity of Shasta Mountain, and further south. A short time afterwards, Doctor Sandels, a very scientific traveler, visited me, and explored a part of the country in a great hurry, as time would not permit him to make a longer stay.

He told me likewise that he found sure signs of gold, and was very sorry that we could not explore the Sierra Nevada. He did not encourage me to attempt to work and open mines, as it was uncertain how it would pay and would probably be only for a government. So I thought it more prudent to stick to the plow, not withstanding I did know that the country was rich in gold, and other minerals. An old attached Mexican servant who followed me here from the United States, as soon as he knew that I was here, and who understood a great deal about working in placers, told me he found sure signs of gold in the mountains on Bear Creek, and that we would go right to work after returning from our campaign in 1845, but he became a victim to his patriotism and fell into the hands of the enemy near my encampment, with dispatches for me from Gen. Micheltorena, and he was hung as a spy, for which I was very sorry.

Ruined by Riches

By this sudden discovery of the gold, all my great plans were destroyed. Had I succeeded for a few years before the gold was discovered, I would have been the richest citizen on the Pacific shore; but it had to be different. Instead of being rich, I am ruined, and the cause of it is the long delay of the United States Land Commission of the United States Courts, through the great influence of the squatter lawyers. Before my case will be decided in Washington, another year may elapse, but I hope that justice will be done me by the last tribunal—the Supreme Court of the United States. By the Land Commission and the District Court it has been decided in my favor. The Common Council of the city of Sacramento, composed partly of squatters, paid Adelpheus Felch (one of the late Land Commissioners, who was engaged by the squatters during his office), $5,000, from the fund of the city, against the will of the tax-payers, for which amount he has to try to defeat my just and old claim from the Mexican government, before the Supreme Court of the United States in Washington.

A Territory Transformed

Walter Colton

The Reverend Walter Colton was serving as a chaplain aboard
the U.S.S. *Congress* when it arrived in California in 1846. For
most of the three years he remained in California, Colton
served as the alcalde, or provincial governor, of Monterey.
After returning to the East Coast in 1850, Colton published
some of his journals and letters in his memoir *Three Years in
California*.

In a May 29, 1848, letter sent to his relatives on the East
Coast, Colton somewhat skeptically reports the news that
gold was discovered on the American Fork of the Sacramento
River. In a subsequent series of letters, the last of which was
dated September 16, 1848, Colton relates the incredible transformation he observed in the area during the short span of
three and a half months after the discovery was confirmed.

MONDAY, MAY 29. Our town was startled out of its quiet
dreams to-day, by the announcement that gold had been
discovered on the American Fork. The men wondered and
talked, and the women too; but neither believed. The sibyls
[fortune-tellers] were less skeptical; they said the moon had,
for several nights, appeared not more than a cable's length
from the earth; that a white raven had been seen playing with
an infant; and that an owl had rung the church bells. . . .

MONDAY, JUNE 5. Another report reached us this morning
from the American Fork. The rumor ran, that several work-

From Walter Colton's diaries published in 1850 as *Three Years in California*.

men, while excavating for a millrace, had thrown up little shining scales of a yellow ore, that proved to be gold; that an old Sonoranian, who had spent his life in gold mines, pronounced it the genuine thing. Still the public incredulity remained, save here and there a glimmer of faith, like the flash of a fire-fly at night. One good old lady, however, declared that she had been dreaming of gold every night for several weeks, and that it had so frustrated her simple household economy, that she had relieved her conscience, by confessing to her priest—

"Absolve me, father, of that sinful dream."

Seeking Verification

TUESDAY, JUNE 6. Being troubled with the golden dream almost as much as the good lady, I determined to put an end to the suspense, and dispatched a messenger this morning to the American Fork. He will have to ride, going and returning, some four hundred miles, but his report will be reliable. We shall then know whether this gold is a fact or a fiction—a tangible reality on the earth, or a fanciful treasure at the base of some rainbow, retreating over hill and waterfall, to lure pursuit and disappoint hope. . . .

MONDAY, JUNE 12. A straggler came in to-day from the American Fork, bringing a piece of yellow ore weighing an ounce. The young dashed the dirt from their eyes, and the old from their spectacles. One brought a spyglass, another an iron ladle; some wanted to melt it, others to hammer it, and a few were satisfied with smelling it. All were full of tests; and many, who could not be gratified in making their experiments, declared it a humbug. One lady sent me a huge gold ring, in the hope of reaching the truth by comparison; while a gentleman placed the specimen on the top of his gold-headed cane and held it up, challenging the sharpest eyes to detect a difference. But doubts still hovered on the minds of the great mass. They could not conceive that such a treasure could have lain there so long undiscovered. The idea seemed to convict them of stupidity. There is nothing of which a man is more tenacious than his claims to sagacity. He sticks to them like an old bachelor to the idea of his personal attractions, or a toper to the strength of his temperance ability, whenever he shall wish to call it into play. . . .

The Fever Strikes

TUESDAY, JUNE 20. My messenger sent to the mines, has returned with specimens of the gold; he dismounted in a sea of upturned faces. As he drew forth the yellow lumps from his pockets, and passed them around among the eager crowd, the doubts, which had lingered till now, fled. All admitted they were gold, except one old man, who still persisted they were some Yankee invention, got up to reconcile the people to the change of flag. The excitement produced was intense; and many were soon busy in their hasty preparations for a departure to the mines. The family who had kept house for me caught the moving infection. Husband and wife were both packing up; the blacksmith dropped his hammer, the carpenter his plane, the mason his trowel, the farmer his sickle, the baker his loaf, and the tapster his bottle. All were off for the mines, some on horses, some on carts, and some on crutches, and one went in a litter. An American woman, who had recently established a boarding-house here, pulled up stakes, and was off before her lodgers had even time to pay their bills. Debtors ran, of course. I have only a community of women left, and a gang of prisoners, with here and there a soldier, who will give his captain the slip at the first chance. I don't blame the fellow a whit; seven dollars a month, while others are making two or three hundred a day! that is too much for human nature to stand.

SATURDAY, JULY 15. The gold fever has reached every servant in Monterey; none are to be trusted in their engagement beyond a week, and as for compulsion, it is like attempting to drive fish into a net with the ocean before them. Gen. Mason, Lieut. Lanman, and myself, form a mess; we have a house, and all the table furniture and culinary apparatus requisite; but our servants have run, one after another, till we are almost in despair: even Sambo [the cook], who we thought would stick by from laziness, if no other cause, ran last night; and this morning, for the fortieth time, we had to take to the kitchen, and cook our own breakfast. A general of the United States Army, the commander of a man-of-war, and the Alcalde [chief administrative officer] of Monterey, in a smoking kitchen, grinding coffee, toasting a herring, and peeling onions! These gold mines are going to upset all the domestic arrangements of society, turning the head to the tail, and the tail to the head. Well, it is an ill wind that blows nobody any good: the nabobs [people of prominence] have had their time, and now comes that of the "niggers." We shall all live just as long, and be quite as fit to die.

Rash Behavior

TUESDAY, JULY 18. Another bag of gold from the mines, and another spasm in the community. It was brought down by a sailor from Yuba river, and contains a hundred and thirty-six ounces. It is the most beautiful gold that has appeared in the market; it looks like the yellow scales of the dolphin, passing through his rainbow hues at death. My carpenters, at work on the school-house, on seeing it, threw down their saws and planes, shouldered their picks, and are off for the Yuba. Three seamen ran from the Warren, forfeiting their four years' pay; and a whole platoon of soldiers from the fort left only their colors behind. One old woman declared she would never again break an egg or kill a chicken, without examining yolk and gizzard. . . .

SATURDAY, AUG. 12. My man Bob, who is of Irish extraction, and who had been in the mines about two months, returned to Monterey four weeks since, bringing with him over two thousand dollars, as the proceeds of his labor. Bob, while in my employ, required me to pay him every Saturday night, in gold, which he put into a little leather bag and sewed into the lining of his coat, after taking out just twelve and a half cents, his weekly allowance for tobacco. But now he took rooms and began to branch out; he had the best horses, the richest viands, and the choicest wines in the place. He never drank himself, but it filled him with delight to brim the sparkling goblet for others. I met Bob to-day, and asked him how he got on. "Oh, very well," he replied, "but I am off again for the mines." "How is that, Bob? you brought down with you over two thousand dollars; I hope you have not spent all that: you used to be very saving; twelve and a half cents a week for tobacco, and the rest you sewed into the lining of your coat." "Oh, yes," replied Bob, "and I have got *that* money yet; I worked hard for it; and the diel can't get it away; but the two thousand dollars came asily by good luck, and has gone as asily as it came." Now Bob's story is only one of a thousand like it in California, and has a deeper philosophy in it than meets the eye. Multitudes here are none the richer for the mines. He who can shake chestnuts from an exhaustless tree, won't stickle about the quantity he roasts.

Instant Riches

THURSDAY, AUG. 16. Four citizens of Monterey are just in from the gold mines on Feather River, where they worked in company with three others. They employed about thirty wild Indians, who are attached to the rancho owned by one of the party. They worked precisely seven weeks and three days, and have divided seventy-six thousand eight hundred and forty-four dollars,—nearly eleven thousand dollars to each. Make a dot there, and let me introduce a man, well known to me, who has worked on the Yuba river sixty-four days, and brought back, as the result of his individual labor, five thousand three hundred and fifty-six dollars. Make a dot there, and let me introduce another townsman, who has worked on the North Fork fifty-seven days, and brought back four thousand five hundred and thirty-four dollars. Make a dot there, and let me introduce a boy, fourteen years of age, who has worked on the Mokelumne fifty-four days, and brought back three thousand four hundred and sixty-seven dollars. Make another dot there, and let me introduce a woman, of Sonoranian birth, who has worked in the dry diggings forty-six days, and brought back two thousand one hundred and twenty-five dollars. Is not this enough to make a man throw down his leger and shoulder a pick? But the deposits which yielded these harvests were now opened for the first time; they were the accumulation of ages; only the footprints of the elk and wild savage had passed over them. Their slumber was broken for the first time by the sturdy arms of the American emigrant.

Social Upheaval

TUESDAY, AUG. 28. The gold mines have upset all social and domestic arrangements in Monterey; the master has become his own servant, and the servant his own lord. The millionaire is obliged to groom his own horse, and roll his wheelbarrow; and the hidalgo—in whose veins flows the blood of all the Cortes—to clean his own boots! Here is lady L—who has lived here seventeen years, the pride and ornament of the place, with a broomstick in her jewelled hand! And here is lady B—with her daughter—all the way from "old Virginia," where they graced society with their varied accomplishments—now floating between the parlor and kitchen, and as much at home in the one as the other! And here is lady S—whose cattle are on a thousand hills, lifting, like Rachel of old, her bucket of water from the deep well! And here is lady M.L.—whose honeymoon is still full of soft seraphic light, un-houseling a potatoe, and hunting the hen that laid the last egg. And here am I, who have been a man of some note in my day, loafing on the hospitality of the good citizens, and grateful for a meal, though in an Indian's wigwam. Why, is not this enough to make one wish the gold mines were in the earth's flaming centre, from which they sprung? Out on this yellow dust! it is worse than the cinders which buried Pompeii, for there, high and low shared the same fate!

SATURDAY, SEPT. 9. I met a Scotchman this morning bent half double, and evidently in pain. On inquiring the cause, he informed me that he had just seen a lump of gold from the Mokelumne as big as his double fist, and it had given him the cholic. The diagnosis of the complaint struck me as a new feature in human maladies, and one for which it would be difficult to find a suitable medicament in the therapeutics known to the profession; especially in the allopathic practice, which has stood still for three thousand years, except in the discovery of quinine for ague [fever with chills], and sulphur for itch. The gentlemen of this embalmed school must wake up; their antediluvian [antiquated] owl may do on an Egyptian obelisk, but we must have a more wide-awake bird in these days of progress. Here is a man bent double with a new and strange disease, taken from looking at gold: your bleeding, blistering, and purging won't free him of it. What is to be done? shall he be left to die, or be delivered over to the homeopathics? They have a medicament that acts as a specific, on the principle that the hair of the dog is good for the bite. If you burn your hand, what do you do—clasp a piece of ice?—no, seize a warm poker; if you freeze your foot, do you put it to the fire?—no, dash it into the snow; and so if you take the gold-cholic, the remedy is, *aurum—similia similibus curantum* [gold—like cures like].

A Democracy of Wealth

SATURDAY, SEPT. 16. The gold mines are producing one good result; every creditor who has gone there is paying his debts. Claims not deemed worth a farthing are now cashed on presentation at nature's great bank. This has rendered the credit of every man here good for almost any amount. Orders for merchandise are honored which six months ago would have been thrown into the fire. There is none so poor, who has two stout arms and a pickaxe left, but he can empty any store in Monterey. Nor has the first instance yet occurred, in which the creditor has suffered. All distinctions indicative of means have vanished; the only capital required is muscle and an honest purpose. I met a man to-day from the mines in patched buckskins, rough as a badger from his hole, who had fifteen thousand dollars in yellow dust, swung at his back. Talk to him of brooches, gold-headed canes, and Carpenter's coats! Why he can unpack a lump of gold that would throw all Chestnut-street into spasms. And there is more where this came from. *His* rights in the great domain are equal to yours, and his prospects of getting it out vastly better. With these advantages, he bends the knee to no man, but strides along in his buckskins, a lord of earth by a higher prescriptive privilege than what emanates from the partiality of kings. His patent is medallioned with rivers which roll over golden sands, and embossed with mountains which have lifted for ages their golden coronets to heaven. Clear out of the way with your crests, and crowns, and pedigree trees, and let this democrat pass. Every drop of blood in his veins tells that it flows from a great heart, which God has made and which man shall never enslave. Such are the genuine sons of California; such may they live and die.

"They will not be the tyrant's slaves,
While heaven has light, or earth has graves."

Reporting to the East Coast

Thomas Larkin

In the spring of 1848, journalist Thomas Larkin was serving in California as a correspondent for the *New York Herald*. When Larkin arrived in San Jose on May 26, he found the townspeople rapt with stories of gold. After penning a letter describing the wild state of affairs to the governor of California, Richard B. Mason, Larkin set off for Sacramento to see for himself if the stories were true.

Larkin found the situation in Sacramento to be almost inconceivable. In two letters to U.S. secretary of state James Buchanan, Larkin strained to contain his exuberance as he described the amazing discoveries of the first miners and the resulting social upheaval in surrounding towns as people abandoned their lives in search of gold. These two letters would be among the first reports of the gold discovery to reach the East Coast of the United States.

THOMAS OLIVER LARKIN, PUEBLO DE SAN JOSE, MAY 26, 1848, TO COLONEL RICHARD B. MASON, GOVERNOR OF CALIFORNIA

Sir

I arrived here after two days travel. Every body is in the greatest state of excitement. We can hear of nothing but Gold, Gold, Gold. An onze [ounce] a day, two a day or three—every one has the gold or yellow fever. Last night several of the most respectible American residents of this town arrived

From Thomas Larkin's letters to Governor Richard B. Mason, in *The Larkin Papers*, vol. 7, pp. 278–79.

home from a visit to the gold regions. Next week they will with their families, and I think nine-tenths of every foreign store keep, mechanic or day labourer of this town and perhaps San Francisco leave for the Sacramento. . . .

Thomas O. Larkin

THOMAS OLIVER LARKIN, SAN FRANCISCO, JUNE 1, 1848, TO THE SECRETARY OF STATE, JAMES BUCHANAN

Sir

I have to report to the State Department one of the most astonishing excitements and state of affairs now existing in this country that perhaps has ever been brought to the notice of the Government. On the American Fork of the Sacramento and Feather River, another branch of the same and the adjoining lands, there has been within the present year discovered a placer, a vast tract of land containing gold in small particles. This gold thus far has been taken on the banks of the river from the surface to eighteen inches in depth and is supposed deeper and to extend over the country. On account of the convenience of washing, the people have to this time only gathered the metal on the banks, which is done simply with a shovel, filling a shallow dish, bowl, basket or tin pan with a quantity of black sand simular to the class used on paper and washing out the sand by movement of the vessel. It is now two or three weeks since the men employed in these washings have appeared in this town with gold to exchange for merchandize and provisions. I presume near twenty thousand dollars ($20,000) of this gold has as yet been so exchanged.

Some two or three hundred of the men have remained up the river or are gone to their homes for the purpose of returning to the Placers and washing immediately with shovels, picks and baskets, many of them for the first few weeks depending on borrowing from others. I have seen the written statement of the work of one man for sixteen days, which averaged twenty five ($25) per day. Others have with a shovel and pan or wooden bowl washed out ten to over fifty dollars in a day. There are now some men yet washing who have five hundred to one thousand dollars. As they have to stand two feet deep in the river, they work but a few hours in the day and not every day in the week.

A Mass Exodus

A few men have been down in boats to this port, spending twenty to thirty ounces of gold each, about three hundred dollars ($300). I am confident that this town (San Francisco) has one half of its tenements empty, locked up with the furniture. The owners—store keepers, lawyers, mechanics and labourers—all gone to the Sacramento with their families. Small parties of five to fifteen men have sent to this town and offered cooks ten to fifteen dollars per day for a few weeks. Mechanics and teamsters earning the year past five to eight dollars per day have struck and gone. Several U.S. Volunteers have deserted. U.S. barque [three-masted ship] Anita, belonging to the Army, now at anchor here, has but six men. One Sandwich Island vessel in port lost all her men, engaged another crew at fifty dollars ($50) for the run of fifteen days to the Islands.

One American captain having his men shipped on this coast in such a manner that they could leave at any time, had them all on the eve of quitting, when he agreed to continue their pay and food, leaving one on board, take a boat and carry them to the gold regions, furnishing tools and giving his men one third. They have been gone a week. Common spades & shovels, one month ago worth one dollar, will now bring ten dollars at the gold regions. I am informed fifty dollars has been offered for one. Should this gold continue as represented, this town and others will be depopulated. Clerks' wages have rose from six hundred to one thousand dollars per annum and board. Cooks twenty five to thirty dollars per month. This sum will not be any inducement a month longer, unless the fever & ague [fever with chills] appears among the washers. The "Californian" printed here stopped this week. The "Star" newspaper office, where the new laws of Govr. Mason for this country is printing, has but one man left. A merchant, lately from China, has even lost his China servants. Should the excitement continue through the year and the whale ships visit San Francisco, I think they will lose most all their crews. How Col. Mason can retain his men unless he puts a force on the spot I know not.

Speculating on the Impact

I have seen several pounds of this gold and consider it very pure, worth in N. York, seventeen to eighteen dollars per ounce. Fourteen to sixteen dollars in merchandise is paid for it here. What good or bad effect this gold region will have on California I can not foretell. It may end this year, but I am informed it will continue many years. Mechanics now in this town are only waiting to finish some rude machinery to enable them to obtain the gold more expeditiously and free from working on the river. Up to this time but few Californians [Mexican residents] have gone to the mines, being afraid the Americans will soon have trouble among themselves and cause disturbance to all around. I have seen some of the black sand as taken from the bottom of the river (I should think in the States it would bring twenty five to fifty cents per pound) containing many pieces of gold. They are from the size of the head of a pin to the weight of the eighth of an ounce. I have seen some weighing one quarter of an ounce (four dollars).

Although my statement is almost incredible I believe I am within the statements believed by every one here. Ten days back the excitement had not reached Monterey. I shall within a few days visit this gold mine and will make another report to you. Enclosed you a specimen. I have the honor to be Very Respectfully

Thomas O. Larkin

P.S. This placer or gold region is situated on public land.

THOMAS OLIVER LARKIN, MONTEREY, JUNE 28, 1848,
TO THE SECRETARY OF STATE, JAMES BUCHANAN

Sir

My last despatch to the State Department was written in San Francisco the first of this month. In that I had the honor to give some information respecting the new "Placer," or gold regions lately discovered on the branches of the Sacremento river. Since the writing of that despatch I have visited a part of the gold regions and found it all I had heard and much more than I anticipated. The part that I visited was upon a fork of the American River, a branch of the Sacremento, joining the main river at Sutter's fort. The place in which I found the people digging was about twenty five miles from the fort by land.

I have reason to believe that gold will be found on many branches of the Sacremento and the Joaquine rivers. People are already scattered over one hundred miles of land, and it is supposed that the "Placer" extends from river to river. At present the workmen are employed within ten or twenty yards of the river, that they may be convenient to water. On Feather River there are several branches upon which the people are digging for gold. This is two or three days ride from the place I visited.

First Observations

At my camping place I found on a surface of two or three miles on the banks of the river some fifty tents, mostly owned by Americans. These had their families. There are no Californians who have taken their families as yet to the gold regions. But few or none will ever do it. Some from New Mexico may do so next year but no Californians. I was two nights at a tent occupied by eight Americans viz [namely] two sailors, one clerk, two carpenters & three daily workmen. These men were in company, had two machines, each made from one hundred feet of boards, worth there one hundred and fifty dollars, in Monterey fifteen dollars, being one days work, made similar to a child's cradle ten feet long without the ends.

The two evenings I saw these eight men bring to their tents the labor of the day, I suppose they made each fifty dollars per day. Their own calculation was two pounds of gold a day, four ounces to a man (sixty four dollars). I saw two brothers that worked together and only worked by washing the dirt in a tin pan, weighed the gold they obtained in one day. The result was seven dollars to one, eighty two dollars the other. There was two reasons for this difference. One man washed less hours in the day than the other and by chance had ground less impregnated with gold. I give this statement as an extreme case.

During my visit I was interpreter for a native of Monterey, who was purchasing a machine or canoe. I first tried to purchase boards and hire a carpenter for him. There was but a few hundred feet of boards to be bad. For these the owner asked me fifty dollars per hundred ($500 per M) and a carpenter washing gold dust demanded fifty dollars per day for working. I at last purchased a log dug out, with a riddle and seive made of willow boughs on it, for one hundred and twenty dollars payable in gold dust at fourteen dollars per ounce. The owner excused himself for the price by saying he was two days making it and even then demanded the use of it until sunset. My Californian has told me since, that himself, partner and two Indians obtained with this canoe eight ounces the first and five ounces the second day.

Current and Future Immigration

I am of the opinion that on the American fork, Feather river, and Cosumes river there are near two thousand people—nine tenths of them foreigners. Perhaps there are one hundred families that have their teams, waggons and tents. Many persons are waiting to see whether the months of July and August will be sickly, before they leave their present business to go to the "Placer." The discovery of this gold was made by some Mormons in [January] or Febuary who for a time kept it a secret. The majority of those who are now working there began in May. In most every instant the men after digging a few days have been compelled to leave for the purpose of returning home to see their families, arrange their business and purchase provision [provisions].

I feel confident in saying there are fifty men in this "Placer" who have on an average one thousand dollars each, obtained in May and June. I have not met with any person who had been fully employed in washing gold one month. Most however appear to have averaged an ounce per day.

I think there must at this time be over one thousand men at work upon the different branches of the Sacremento. Putting their gains at ten thousand per day for six days in the week appears to me not overrated. Should this news reach the emigration of California and Origon [Oregon] now on the road, connected with the Indian wars, now impoverishing the latter country, we should have a large addition to our population, and should the richness of the gold region continue, our emigration in 1849 will be many thousand and in 1850 still more. If our country men in California as clerks, mechanics & workmen will forsake employment at from two to six dollars per day, how many more of the same class in the Atlantic states earning much less will leave for this country under such prospects. It is the opinion of many who have visited the gold regions the past and present months that the grounds will afford gold for many years perhaps for a century. From my own examination of the rivers and their banks I am of opinion that at least for a few years the golden products will equal the present year. However as neither men of science nor the laborers now at work have made any explorations of consequence it is a matter of impossibility to give any opinion as to the extent and richness of this part of California. Every Mexican who has seen the place says throughout their Republic there has never been any placer like this one.

Astounding but True

Could Mr. Polk and yourself see California as we now see it, you would think that a few thousand people on one hundred miles square of the Sacremento Valley would yearly turn out of this river the whole price our country pays for all the acquired territory. When I finished my first letter I doubted my own writing and to be better satisfied showed it to one of the principle merchants of San Francisco and to Capt. Folsom of the [Quarter] Master's Department who decided at once I was far below the reality. You certainly will suppose from my two letters that I am like others led away by the excitement of the day. I think I am not. In my last I enclosed a small sample of the gold dust and find my only error was in putting a value to the sand. At that time I was not aware how the gold was found. I now can describe the mode of collecting it. A person with[out] a machine after digging off one or two feet of upper ground near the water (in some cases they take the top earth) throw into a tin pan or wooden bowl a shovel full of loose dirt and stones, then placing the basin an inch under water continue to stir up the dirt with his hand in such a manner that the running water will, carry off the light earth, occasionally with his hand throwing out the stones. After an operation of this kind for twenty or thirty minutes, they find a spoon full of emaral [emery] black sand remains. This is on a [handkerchief] or cloth dried in the sun. When dried the emery is blown off leaving the pure gold.

I have the pleasure of enclosing a paper of this sand and gold which I from a bucket of dirt and stones in half hour standing at the edge of the water washed out myself. The value of it may be two or three dollars. The size of the gold depends in some measure upon the river from which it is taken, the banks of one river having larger grains of gold than another. I presume more than one half of the gold put into pans or machines is washed out and goes down the stream. This is of no consequence to the washers who care only for the present time. Some have formed companies of four or five men and have a rough made machine put together in a day which works to much advantage, yet many prefer to work alone with a wooden bowl or tinpan worth fifteen or twenty cents in the States but eight to sixteen dollars at the gold regions. As the workmen continue and materials can be obtained improvements will take place in the mode of obtaining gold. At present it is obtained by standing in the water and with much severe labor, or such as is called here severe labor.

An Extraordinary State of Affairs

How long this gathering of gold by the handfulls will continue here or the future effects it will have on California I cannot say. Three fourths of the houses in the town on the bay of San Francisco are deserted. Houses are sold at the price of the ground lots. The effects are this week showing themselves in Monterey. Almost every house I had hired out is given up. Every blacksmith, carpenter and lawyer are leaving. Brick yards, sawmills and ranches are left perfectly alone. A large number of the volunteers at San Francisco and Sonoma have deserted. Some have been retaken and brought back. Public and private vessels are losing their crews. My clerks have had one hundred per cent advance offered them on their wages to accept employment. A complete revolution in the ordinary state of affairs is taking place. Both of our newspapers are discontinued from want of workmen and the loss of their agencies. The Alcaldes [chief administrative officers] have left San Francisco and I believe Sonoma likewise. The former place has not a justice of the peace left. The second Alcalde of Monterey to day joins the keepers of our principal hotel who have closed their office and house and will leave tomorrow for the golden rivers. I saw on the ground a lawyer who was last year Attorney General for the King of the Sandwich Islands, digging and washing over his ounce and a half per day. Near him can be found most all his brethren of the long robe working in the same occupation.

To conclude, my letter is long but I could not well describe what I have seen in less words, and I now can believe that my account may be doubled. If the affair proves a bauble—a mere excitement, I know not how we can all be deceived as we are situated. Gov. Mason and his staff have left Monterey to visit the place in question and will I suppose soon forward to his Department his views and opinions on this subject. Most of the land where the gold has been discovered is public land. There are on different rivers some private grants. I have three such purchased in 1846 and 47, but have not learnt that any private lands have produced gold, though they may hereafter do so. I have the honor, Dear Sir, to be Very Respectfully, Your Obt. Sevt [Obedient Servant].

Thomas O. Larkin

Hon. James Buchanan, Sec. of State
Washington City

Chapter 2

The Rush: Heading Westward

Chapter Preface

A t the time gold fever began to spread across the country in late 1848, most Americans lived along the Eastern seaboard. If they wished to make their way to California for a chance at instant wealth, they had two choices— make the long overland journey across the three-thousand-mile breadth of North America or take the sea route around the tip of South America.

Most chose to travel by ship from eastern ports, but the trip was by no means uncomplicated. The ocean voyage often took over six months, and the notoriously rough seas at Cape Horn gave rise to dangerous passage. Many of the passengers suffered from chronic seasickness and lack of good nutrition: Food often became rancid, and fresh water contaminated, during the long stretches at sea.

Desire to reach the gold fields faster yielded a quicker route across Central America. Ships began sailing to the Gulf Coast of Panama, where passengers would disembark and make their way across the isthmus to the Pacific Ocean. Traversing the wild rain forests of the country's interior, however, was perilous and slow, with travelers risking exposure to potentially fatal diseases such as malaria, cholera, and yellow fever. And there was no guarantee that ships would be available at the Pacific ports to ferry the forty-niners up the coast to San Francisco. Many travelers ran out of money along the way and found themselves in limbo in a foreign land.

For those who lived in the central United States, it was impractical to travel to the East or Gulf Coasts to book passage by ship, only to spend another four to six months at sea. Most midwesterners therefore chose to travel to California by land across the desolate plains, mountains, and deserts of the west. Wagon trains departed from the outposts of Missouri and largely followed the previously established Oregon-California trail. Although the overland route was much shorter in actual distance than the sea route, it usually required the same six months to complete.

Tales of Indian savageness stirred the fears of travelers, but most tribes encountered along the route were peaceful. The wilderness was not without perils, however. Sickness and malnutrition claimed some travelers, while others were forced to turn back to civilization out of a simple inability to tolerate the everyday drudgery of the trip. Because most parties were forced to wait out the winter before departing, they often reached the western deserts in middle of summer, when water was scarce. Those unlucky enough to be in short supply were occasionally forced to pay as much as $100 for a single drink. Some unfortunates who could not pay the high price were actually left to die in the desert heat.

Leaving It All Behind

Edward W. McIlhany

Early in 1849, twenty-year-old Edward W. McIlhany was struck by the gold fever spreading across the United States and the world. He left his native West Virginia that spring with nothing but a chance that he might be allowed to join a mining company already formed in Charleston, Virginia. Fortunately for McIlhany, his luck began before he ever departed for California: He was the last of five newcomers added to the group after the members decided at the last minute to expand their ranks.

Unlike many other forty-niners who departed from the East Coast by ship, McIlhany made the long, arduous journey across the nation's interior by wagon train with his company. He eventually reached California, where he prospected for gold at Grass Valley and on the Feather River. He later opened a general store and hotel in Onion Valley before leaving California for the ensuing Colorado gold rush.

In the following excerpt from his book *Recollections of a Forty-Niner*, McIlhany recounts the strange mixture of enthusiasm and melancholy that was common in those, like him, who were leaving home and family behind for the dream of gold in California.

A t the age of 20, the great discovery of gold in California fired my heart with ambition to see the wild, wild west, and as Horace Greely advised, "Go west, young man, go west and grow up with the country." One motive which

From Edward W. McIlhany, *Recollections of a Forty-Niner* (Kansas City, MO: Hailman, 1908).

caused this desire was disappointment in my first love affair, and I wanted to get far, far away, and try to forget. I welcomed the lines of the poet,

> There is a pleasure in the pathless woods,
> There is a rapture on the lonely shore,
> There is society where none intrude,
> By the deep sea, and music in its roar.

Hearing of a company being formed in Charleston, Jefferson County, Virginia, ten miles west of Harper's Ferry, the place where John Brown made his raid to free the slaves, I realized that here was the opportunity.

Joining Other Dreamers

The company who was formed was to start to California March 3rd, 1849. There were three men from my neighborhood that had joined this company, and one of these men, Ed Hooper, was going to Charleston to pay his dues, so I went with him to try to join the same party. We rode horseback, and forded the Shenandoah River. He rode a large horse, mine was small, and about half way across, my horse commenced swimming, and swam to shore. I was soaking wet from head to foot but happy in the thought that my hopes might soon be realized. Hooper made fun of me but said, "Mc, you have nerve enough to make a good one across the plains." We reached Charleston by night and stopping at a hotel, ate a hearty supper as you can imagine. There were about fifty guests at the hotel, most of whom had come to try to join the company. They asked how I came to be so wet. I told them I had swum the river in my anxiety to join the company. They were amused and remarked, "You've got nerve," and said also, "We are here for the purpose of joining the company. We fear, however, we are too late, as we have been informed the quota of seventy-five is full." My heart fell.

These men were mostly farmers and mechanics with a few lawyers whose limited practice bespoke a change. The company was desirous of having strong, able bodied men, who could endure the hardships of such an adventure, without shrinking. The company was thoroughly organized, and during the conversation that night, they decided to hold a meeting next morning to see if they could increase the number. The meeting was held and voted to increase it only five more, which made it eighty men. The company was then complete.

Forty of these applicants were made to stand in a row to be examined physically, and I fortunately was the fifth and last one to be taken on, which naturally gave me great joy. I then went to the secretary and gave him the $300.00 required to become a member of the company, which was called the Charleston, Jefferson County, Virginia, Mining Company. Each member was given a rubber sack with the company's mark on it, to use in carrying his clothing. The 3rd of March, 1849, a day never to be forgotten, was the date set for our departure. I returned to my home, reached there as the family was eating supper and threw my sack on the floor remarking that I was a member of the company destined to cross the plains to California.

A Difficult Departure

Still bouyant with hope and anticipation the date for starting came and I bade a sad farewell to my family and reached Charleston in time to join my company on March 3rd. There were hundreds of our friends to bid us good-bye. Fathers, mothers, brothers, sisters, wives, sweethearts and even old family darkies—all with tears in their eyes for they knew not our way.

Although it was March, generally a stormy month, that day was calm and beautiful. Still we were sad at the thought that perhaps we might never see our loved ones again.

A special train was to bear us to Harper's Ferry. The baggage was put aboard. The engine was quietly puffing with steam up. The bell rang, the conductor called, "All aboard," then the parting, a tragic scene such as I want never to witness again.

We reached Harper's Ferry at noon. Then we took the Baltimore Ohio Railroad to Cumberland, Maryland, the terminus of the road at that time. Father met me at Harper's Ferry, with tears in his eyes, the first I ever saw him shed. He said, "My son, here is a hymn book and a bible from your mother and myself. I would rather give you $1,000.00 than to have you leave me today," but I replied, "Father, it is for the best."

Passage by Sea

Enos Christman

In July of 1849, twenty-year-old Enos Christman of West Chester, Pennsylvania, had much to be thankful for. He had apprenticed himself as a printer at the town's *Village Record* newspaper. He had a loving fiancée named Ellen Apple, and he had developed good friends, including his most loyal, Peebles Prizer. But like many other wide-eyed young men of his day, he decided to leave his job, his friends, and his love behind for a chance at California gold.

Christman joined the California Gold Mining Company of Philadelphia that summer and outfitted himself for the journey to California. Like many others on the East Coast of the United States, he embarked by ship rather than wagon train. His journey would eventually take him around the Horn of South America and on to San Francisco. Christman made it to the gold fields of California, and after some success prospecting in the mines, he partnered in the publication of the *Herald* newspaper in Sonoma from 1850 to 1852. He returned to West Chester in 1853 a richer man and made good on his promise to marry his sweetheart Ellen.

At Ellen's request, Christman maintained a journal of his travels during the four years he was away from West Chester. His reporting skills having been honed by his experience at the *Village Record* and the *Sonoma Herald*, Christman meticulously recorded his experiences in his journal. He also preserved letters to and from Ellen, his old boss, and his friend Peebles, whom he had entrusted to look after Ellen during his absence. For three-quarters of a century, these documents lay in a tin box in a closet under the stairway of the Christman

From Enos Christman, *One Man's Gold: The Letters and Journal of a Forty-Niner*, edited by Florence M. Christman (New York: Whittlesby House, McGraw-Hill, 1930). Reprinted by permission of the McGraw-Hill Companies.

family home. Once discovered, the writings were edited and published by Enos's descendant Florence M. Christman in the book *One Man's Gold: The Letters and Journal of a Forty-Niner*. In the following excerpt, Christman recounts his emotional departure from Philadelphia and his passage out to sea.

W e left Pine Street Wharf, Philadelphia, on Tuesday evening, July 3, 1849, amid the shouts and cheers of assembled hundreds and anchored below the Navy Yard until next morning. In order to complete some necessary repairs, we were detained in the Delaware River and Bay until Saturday afternoon, July 7th, when the steamer which towed us down the river left us at the Capes. After passing the breakwater we soon lost sight of land, and as the green hills and trees disappeared, a melancholy sensation seized upon us as we reflected that this might be the last time we would be permitted to gaze upon the beautiful hills and vales of our native land. This sensation soon wore away, however, as we came to look around and beheld nothing but the heaving ocean stretched out before us and the blue sky above. This, to one unaccustomed to the like, was a sight at once grand and imposing. Toward the end of the day, many of the passengers began to get seasick and I felt a little squeamish myself. I turned in, however, early and slept soundly until morning, when I too was seized with the prevailing epidemic.

Conflicted Emotions of Departure

My feelings and emotions on leaving my friends and my native land on such an expedition, I cannot describe. I have left all that is near and dear and turned my face towards a strange land, expecting to be absent two or three years, hoping in that time to realize a fortune; and then return and be greeted by kind friends. And this hope is my greatest consolation and comfort. Often memory carries me back to the *Record* office, and were I of a desponding temperament, I should wish myself there again. But hope whispers all is well, and so I proceed with a strong arm and an honest heart, with bright anticipations of joy and happiness in the future. But why do I predict anything? Lofty castles have oft been built in the air and a single rude breath sufficed to level them to the earth.

The ship is owned and fitted out by G.W. Hathaway Co. of Philadelphia. They advertised accommodations for first and second cabin passengers, the former at $200 and the latter at $160. Thirty of the passengers are members of the California Gold Mining Association of Philadelphia, of which I am one, as well as my friend, DeWitt Clinton Atkins. They are as merry a set of fellows as ever sailed. Our Association engaged 2nd cabin passage with Mr. N.B. Finley, the agent of Hathaway Co., and by him they were assured that they would be furnished the same fare as the first cabin passengers, and that the difference in price was made in consequence of the first cabin passengers being furnished with everything, while the lower cabin passengers furnished their own bedding and table furniture, and occupied the cabin between decks. A contract was drawn up enumerating the articles and quantity of food to be allowed each one in the lower cabin.

Our Association is divided into five sections. I am director of Section No. 5 which consists of six men. We each paid thirty dollars and purchased the following for use after arrival in San Francisco: 3 bbls. [barrels] pilot bread, 2 do. [dozen] pork, 1/2 do. beef, 1 do. beans, 1 do. vinegar, one tent fourteen feet square, axe, hatchet, 2 spades, 2 shovels, 2 picks, 10 lbs. nails, pots, kettles, pans, table furniture, gum oversuit.

Outfitted for the West

My personal outfit I bought with the money furnished me by Mr. Evans upon my departure. He is to receive fifty per cent of my earnings for two years after my arrival in California, in payment for the outfit as well as for six months' service which I owe him as apprentice. I have everything I can think of and over fifty dollars of my own in my pocket. As near as I can recollect at this time, the following com-

Travelers enjoy fair weather on the deck of a ship headed to California. As ships neared Cape Horn, the weather often grew stormy and cold.

prises what I have brought with me: One government rifle, one navy pistol, one small rifle pistol, belt for same; six lbs. powder, six lbs. balls, 1,500 caps, large bowie knife, 17 pairs new heavy pantaloons, 12 new flannel shirts, 18 new checked shirts, five white muslin shirts, seven coats, five waistcoats, six new cotton neck cloths, 8 pairs of boots, shoes and slippers, four hats and caps, 18 pairs stockings, one nightcap, combs, brushes; ten lbs. of lead for casting bullets, six jars of pickles, one bottle of blackberry syrup, one lb. essence of beef, box of fresh water soap, do. of salt water, 3 lbs. of loaf sugar, peppermint, camphor, sulphur and brimstone, laudanum, twine, ropes, shaving apparatus, table knife, fork, spoon, plate, tin cup, iron frying pan, wash basin, etc.; a variety of books and stationery; bed and bedding, a bundle of rags and a box of all-healing salve.

Should I ever ship again I would take the following additional articles: Two or three dozen of mineral water, box of raisins, and a few other delicacies for use during seasickness. In addition to the articles mentioned in the foregoing list, I have taken a gallon of best fourth-proof brandy which I intend as medicine and for emergencies. We have given up to our Captain, Addison Palmer, all our arms and ammunition for safekeeping. He seems to be a whole-souled sort of fellow.

Life at Sea

We have about fifty-one passengers on board, among whom are six lady passengers, one little boy three years old and one infant at its mother's breast. Three of the ladies are in our cabin. This will add much to our social comforts, for without the smiles of women nothing can prosper.

Today the passengers are all busily engaged in curing a lot of cabbage bought for their own convenience. Our fare is pretty hard, but as we are not quite regulated yet, more of this anon. I believe I am the only male passenger out of over forty who is free from the vice of using tobacco, either smoking or chewing. Some play cards or dominoes to while away the time. All, I believe, are supplied with books and many are commencing journals. All are disposed to minister to the comfort of others. So far we have progressed as a band of brothers and have had a delightful passage except that many of us have been seasick. DeWitt and I were miserable, indeed, but are recovering slowly. One of the sailors on board who had been sick and in a melancholy mood stabbed himself in the breast. He was taken on shore at New Castle, Delaware, and sent to Philadelphia. We fear he cannot recover.

On the evening of the Fourth of July, the Declaration of Independence was read by R.C. Stockton. Fiddling and dancing accompanied by drinking were kept up nearly all night. Next day some of the passengers, in consequence of the proceedings of the previous night, slept nearly all day.

We have not yet [passed near] a vessel and feel as if we were a little isolated community floating all alone on the broad bosom of the Atlantic, but we raised our colors to let two vessels in the distance know we were American. One was home bound, the other from some foreign port.

Following our vessel are quite a number of birds resembling our common barnswallow, called Mother Carey's chicks, which, it is said, will follow us until we reach Cape

Horn. While in the river we espied numerous sturgeons jumping out of the water, displaying their full length. Since we have come into the Atlantic we have seen many porpoises which appear about as large as full-grown hogs—the best comparison I can make, never having seen one except as they rise on the surface of the water.

Into the Wild Plains

David R. Leeper

When a small party of six men set out from South Bend, Indiana for the gold fields of California on February 22, 1849, the glamour of their endeavor generated considerable local interest. Many friends and spectators gathered to see them away as they rolled out of town in two covered wagons. Filled with the spirit of adventure, the men joined in the chorus of the popular gold rush song of the time:

Oh, California!
That's the land for me;
I'm going to Sacramento
With a washbowl on my knee.

The oldest of the young men in the party was twenty-five. Like the others in the group, the youngest, David R. Leeper, would soon discover just how unromantic the journey westward could be. Departing in the middle of the spring thaw, the party was almost immediately bogged down on muddy roads. Because many streams and rivers had overflowed their banks, the men were additionally slowed by washed-out bridges and flooded lowlands. In order to keep their progress, the men were many times forced to make wide detours and to ford rivers along the way.

After almost three months of laborious travel, the group reached St. Joseph, Missouri, which was then the western edge of civilization. When the men left the outpost on May 16, the great plains, mountains, and deserts of the West still lay before them. In the following except from his book *The Argonauts of 'Forty-Nine*, Leeper recounts his experiences as his party encountered the wilderness expanse.

From David R. Leeper, *The Argonauts of 'Forty-Nine* (South Bend, IN: Stoll & Co., 1894).

St. Joseph, Missouri, was our objective point on the frontier. We found this border city—the last outpost of civilization—thronged with gold-seekers like ourselves. They had flocked hither from every quarter to fit out for the overland journey. Many had pushed out before our arrival; many were still coming in; and all was hurry-scurry with excitement. The only transportation available for crossing the Missouri River was a big clumsy scow or flat-boat propelled by long oars or sweeps. We chartered this craft for one night, several parties clubbing with us for the purpose. The price stipulated was ninety dollars, we to perform the labor. The task was by no means a holiday diversion. I tugged at the end of one of those sweeps myself all night, and it seemed a long, long night, indeed. The Big Muddy was booming from the spring freshets, and at this point hurled its entire volume sheer against a precipitous bluff just above the ferrying-place, thus lashing its waters, ordinarily very violent, into redoubled fury. But we were equal to the emergency, and succeeded in placing the turbulent flood behind [us]. . . .

Into the Wilderness

On May 16, we pulled out from the Missouri River through the muddy timbered bottom to the open bluffs. We had now, sure enough, bid adieu to civilization. The wild beast and the sportive, hair-lifting savage rose up in grim visions before us. . . . Over two thousand miles of this sort of forbidding prospect lay before us. A strong force and a rigid discipline were very naturally conceived of as the imperative needs of the hour. Many emigrants—as we were all denominated [known] at that time—were encamped about us, and all were impressed with a like portentous [ominous] sense of the situation. We were, therefore, not long in marshaling a train of some sixty wagons, duly equipped with officers and a bristling code of rules. Guards were to pace their beats regularly of nights, and the stock was all to be carefully corralled by arranging the wagons in the form of an enclosure for this purpose. Johnson Horrell, who was for many years a conspicuous figure in the history of South

Bend, was given the chief command. As we pushed out from the river bluffs into the open country beyond, our long line of "prairie schooners" looked sightly indeed, as it gracefully wound itself over the green, billowy landscape. . . .

Overburdened with Supplies

We had not been out many days beyond the confines of civilization, when, in a stroll some distance from the train, I discovered a good wagon tire.

Such reckless abandonment of property was something new to me. I rolled the valuable article along for a while, striving vigorously to reach the moving train with it, but had at last to abandon the effort in despair. From about this time onward, we saw castaway articles strewn by the roadside one after another in increasing profusion till we could have taken our choice of the best of wagons . . . with much of their [load intact], had we been provided with the extra teams to draw them. Some of the draft animals perished, some stampeded, and all became more or less jaded and foot-worn. One train, from Columbus, Ohio, lost every animal it had through that inexplicable fright known as stampede. Hence the means for transportation became inadequate thus early on the journey, and were every day becoming more and more reduced. Many of the emigrants had provided enough supplies to last them a year or two; but they were not long in seeing the propriety, if not the actual necessity, of reducing their [load] as much as possible, with the view both of relieving their teams and facilitating their progress. Even the wagon boxes were in many cases shortened, and tons upon tons of bacon and other articles of the outfits were converted into fuel, the main purpose being to favor the teams.

Fuel was quite an object through that part of the route now known as Nebraska and Eastern Wyoming. On the lower part of the main Platte [River], [finding] wood was somewhat [difficult]. . . .

For a number of days, a heavy belt of cottonwoods was temptingly near at hand; but not in a single instance were

we able to reach a trunk, limb, or twig because of an inter-
vening section of the river. Weeds and buffalo "chips" . . .
were about our only resource, and the latter, I may say,
made an excellent fuel when it could be had. To husband
[conserve] as much as possible the scanty supply of such
fuel as was obtainable, we improvised a sort of furnace by
cutting a narrow trench in the sod so that the coffee-pot and
frying-pan would span the breadth of the fire and rest upon
the walls of the opening. Coffee, flapjacks and bacon were
about the only articles we had to prepare, and in the turning
or "flipping" of the flapjacks, especially, we soon became
very expert.

An Emotionally Taxing Journey

As to our grand caravan, it steadily came to grief. The inex-
pediency of traveling in so large a body became more and
more manifest [obvious] as we approached the mountains,
and the rough roads and difficult passages delayed progress
by the necessity of one team having to wait on another, especially where the doubling of teams was required. Other in-
fluences tended to the same end. As we became accustomed
to the plains, our wariness from visions of the tomahawk and
the scalping-knife gradually wore away into . . . indifference,
so that we cared nothing for the security that numbers might
afford. I carried no arms, yet often wandered miles away
from the train alone as this or that object might happen to at-
tract my attention. The parching winds and stifling dust, with
the . . . blotched and blistered lips that afflicted nearly every
one in consequence, did not at all [contribute to] that ge-
niality of temper that would incline men to social solace. Besides, on the earlier part of the route, there was much sickness, and many deaths occurred, which occasioned
annoyances and delays irksome to those not immediately interested. It is not very strange, therefore, that, with all these
dismembering tendencies at work, our once imposing
pageant should have so ingloriusly faded that before we had
fairly reached the mountains it had passed into "innocuous
desuetude [harmless disuse]." Even our own little party un-

derwent depletions from time to time until but three members of the original six remained. These three traveled and camped alone for many days, with the utmost unconcern as to whether anybody else was far or near. As for keeping watch, all thought of that had vanished before we had proceeded a quarter of our way. Tents, too, were early abandoned as useless luxuries, and each individual when retiring for the night, sought out the most eligible site he could find (usually among the sage-brush), and rolling himself up in his blankets and buffalo robes thus committed himself to the "sweet restorer," with only the starry canopy for a shelter. . . .

Hunting Wild Game

Game was by no means as plentiful as one would have supposed. We found more of it in the states through which we passed than in the country beyond. In the region now known as Nebraska many antelopes were seen bounding over the plain or watching our movements from elevated points; but they were shy, vigilant, and hard to capture. In the mountains, deer and mountain sheep . . . were occasionally sighted and brought down, and when we struck the magnificent pasture ranges of California, deer, elk, antelope and bear abounded. At the "Big Meadows," on Feather River, where we lay by several days to recruit our oxen, Neal brought in seven blacktail deer in one day. I was out at the same time equally eager on the chase, but the game did not appear at all enamored of my presence, so I had my ammunition for my pains. But, on the whole, our banquets on the luxuries of the chase were few and far between. Strange to say, we saw but few buffaloes (properly bison), not more than a dozen or so, all told. Those few we saw near where we forded the South Platte.

Crossing the Isthmus of Panama

Mary Jane Megquier

In January 1849, Winthrop, Maine, resident Dr. Thomas L. Megquier and a few of his associates were planning to try their fortunes in California. Having had limited success in Winthrop, Dr. Megquier hoped to open a medical practice and drug store in the boom town of San Francisco. Noting that his long days of labor in Winthrop had not provided adequate compensation to redress his accumulated debts, Megquier's wife, Mary Jane, was supportive of the venture.

At the last minute, Dr. Megquier and his associates elected to take Mary Jane with them. With "women's work" being difficult to fill in a growing city like San Francisco, the men believed that she would be compensated well there. Mary Jane was more than willing to go on the venture, but her enthusiasm was somewhat tempered by the necessity that she leave her children behind to stay with relatives.

The Megquiers and their party departed from New York on March 1, 1849, and after a passage of twelve days reached the harbor of Chagres, Panama. Mary was the only woman among the two hundred passengers aboard the ship. In the following selection from her book *Apron Full of Gold*, which chronicles her travels in a series of letters to family and friends, Mary describes her journey across the primitive Isthmus of Panama. She and her husband eventually reached San Francisco, where she successfully ran a boarding house.

From *Apron Full of Gold: The Letters of Mary Jane Megquier from San Francisco, 1849–1856*, edited by Robert Glass Cleland. Copyright © 1949 by the Henry E. Huntington Library and Art Gallery. Reprinted with permission of the Henry E. Huntington Library.

May 14, 1849

D ear friend Milton,
     Thinking you might like to hear of our whereabouts,
I will try and rub open my eyes and tell you some of our
journeyings, but it is an effort, as the climate is such that I
cannot keep the day of the week. But to our journey: We
started from New York the first day of March. After a very
pleasant passage of twelve days we landed at Chagres, a
small village of about six hundred inhabitants living in huts
built of bamboo poles supported by pieces of timber and
covered with grass and palm leaves. At the left, as you enter the harbor, is a fine old castle built of stone by the buc-
caneers. It commands the whole harbor; it is surrounded by
a moat and a high wall on which you can see the guns peeping at you. Many have fallen from their places; others will
keep theirs for years to come. A negro is the only tenant. I
think he is getting rich by charging one rial for admission.
The Americans all rush to it in a perfect frenzy, but it very
soon abates after living in Panama a while. As you pass
along the village you will see the Astor House [and] still farther the Crescent City Hotel, where you get beef and fish by
the yard [and] stewed monkeys and iguanoes, but my ap-
petite has not been quite sharp enough to relish those yet.

Into the Wild

The natives are cleanly in their person and dress. They are
a simple inoffensive people but understand perfectly the getting of the dimes from the Americans. After stopping a few
hours we started on the steamboat Orus with about thirty canoes attached to the stern . . . to take us to Gorgona from the
head of steamboat navigation, which in the dry season is
only sixteen miles, to a small village called the Twin Sisters,
where we spent the night. It was a rich scene to see one hundred and fifty Americans crowded on to a boat the size of
the celebrated Phoenix, some trying to get a cup of coffee,
others a [place] to lie, but at last we got a chance to rest for
a couple of hours, before all was bustle and confusion again

in making preparation for our journey up the river. Our breakfast [was] a cup of miserable coffee and hard bread.

After waiting three or four hours we were stowed into a canoe (Mr. Calkin, Dr. [Megquier] and myself) twenty feet long [and] two feet wide with all our luggage, which brought the top of the canoe very near the water's edge. We seated ourselves on our carpet bags on the bottom of the boat; if we attempted to alter our position, we were sure to get wet feet. Notwithstanding our close quarters, the scenery was so delightful—the banks covered with the most beautiful shrubbery and flowers, trees as large as our maple covered with flowers of every color and hue, birds of all descriptions filled the air with music, while the monkeys, alligators and other animals varied the scene—that we were not conscious of fatigue. Two natives pushed the boat with poles; [when] the water was too swift for them, they would step out very deliberately and pull us along. . . . There are ranchos every few miles where you can get a cup of miserable muddy coffee with hard bread, of which we made dinner. Then we doubled ourselves in as small [a group] as possible and started, under a broiling sun—the thermometer at one hundred. [We] arrived at our destination for the night about five o'clock, where we seated ourselves on the bank to watch the arrival of the canoes. Before dark there were one hundred Americans on that small spot of ground, all busy as bees making preparation for the night. Our party thought it best to have the natives cook . . . supper; it was rich to see us eating soup with our fingers, as knives, forks, spoons, tables, [and] chairs are among the things unknown. They have no floors; the pigs, dogs, cats, ducks, [and] hens are all around your feet ready to catch the smallest crumb that may chance to fall. As I was the only lady in the party, they gave me a chance in their hut, but a white lady was such a rare sight they were coming in to see me until we found we could get no sleep. We got up and spent the remainder of the night in open air. At four we took up our bed and walked; would to God I could describe the scene. The birds singing, monkeys screeching, the Americans laughing and joking, [and] the na-

Survival at Sea

Henry V. Huntley, a British naval officer and colonial administrator, was stationed in San Francisco in 1852 as the representative of a British gold and quartz mining company. His book California: Its Gold and Its Inhabitants *captures his observations of California business and social life during his stay.*

In the following excerpt, Huntley discusses the mortal risk involved in traveling to California by way of Panama. The Isthmus crossing alone brought with it the risk of contracting potentially fatal diseases, such as cholera and yellow fever, and the ensuing cramped steamer voyage only served to exacerbate any afflictions already suffered by the passengers.

The steamers "S.S. Louis" and "Tennessee" have recently arrived from Panama.

On board the first, during the passage of fourteen or fifteen days, forty deaths occurred, and on board the other, thirty-four.

This mortality originates in the climate of the Isthmus, and is rendered fatal by embarcation on board the American steam-vessels running between Panama and San Francisco.

These vessels frequently carry a thousand passengers at a trip. The steerage passengers are packed together little better than negroes are on board slave ships; they lie on shelves one over the other; are often very ill fed, sometimes even water is stinted, although the passage is so short; and the ventilation is poorly provided for.

They have a person on board termed a surgeon, or rather, the doctor, who, as far as experience goes, I must say, is neither attentive nor capable. In point of fact, the only effort of the company owning these vessels is to gain the greatest number of dollars for the least amount of outlay; once pay your fare, and you are no longer worth consideration.

Henry V. Huntley, *California: Its Gold and Its Inhabitants*. London: T.C. Newby, 1856.

tives grunting as they pushed us along through the rapids were enough to drive one mad with delight. . . .

A Primitive Outpost

At four in the evening we reached Gorgona, another miserable town, where you will find the French, New York, and California Hotels but you cannot get decent food, nor a bed to lie upon at either house. There is a church in town which is not as respectable as the meanest barn you have in town. They have the ruin of a bell, the tongue of another, hung three feet from the ground, with the addition of a drum made by drawing a bit of hide over the ends of a small keg, which the little negroes use to good advantage in calling the congregation together. They divide [the church] off with raw hides to prevent being overrun with domestic animals in time of service. A mule took the liberty to depart this life within its walls while we were there, which was looked upon by the natives [as] of no consequence.

After spending two nights and a day at Gorgona, we resumed our journey for Panama [City] on the backs of the most miserable apologies for horse flesh that you could conceive of. They were completely exhausted carrying heavy loads over one of the roughest roads in the world, nothing but a path wide enough for the feet of the mule, which if he should make a misstep, you would go to parts unknown. Many places were so narrow it would be impossible to pass each other on horse back. The muleteer would give the alarm that they might stop on the opposite side. On the top of one of those high hills we found [a young American] dishing out beans, coffee, and pancakes in a comfortable way; as there was no way of getting to California, he thought he [would] make a little money where he was. At five in the evening the towers of Panama [City] showed themselves in the distance. I assure you they were hailed with joy after a fatiguing ride of 24 miles. Panama [City] is an old Spanish town, the houses built of stone, whitewashed outside, the roofs covered with tile. On the first floor [there is] a large entrance where you ride to the foot of the stairs, which takes you to the second story, where there are large doors opening onto a verandah from every room. They have no windows or chimnies, [and cooking is done] on a platform built for the purpose. . . . There are a great number of churches, each having quite a number of bells, which they contrive to keep some one thumping most of the time. In the inside you will see some of the good folks of olden time dressed in gaudy silks and satins, but the most conspicuous is the Virgin Mary holding the little Jesus covered with dirty laces and some splendid diamonds peeping out from among the cobwebs. . . . The town is surrounded by a wall twenty feet high and as many feet thick; on the water side it is surmounted by enormous big guns weighing two or three tons, which the Americans have worn quite smooth sitting astride them looking for the steamer. . . .

It used to make my blood chill when I read of our soldiers in the Mexican war finding scorpions in their boots, but I have learned by experience that it is a trifling affair. Besides, I have had jiggers in my feet, a small insect that lays its eggs in your flesh, but all these things are nothing when you get used to them.

May 20, 1849

When we arrived here we did not expect to stay but a short time, [but] for want of coal, the steamers have been detained, until two weeks ago when the Panama and Oregon arrived, one from California, the other around Cape Horn. The passengers [have] been pouring in from the states all the while until the town was overrun, but a great number of sailing vessels have been in and taken them nearly all. If it were not for the uncertainty which is hanging around us, I should [have] enjoyed it very well I assure you. There is a great deal of excitement, which you are well aware I enjoy. The Dr. has done nearly business enough to pay our expense, which is $18 per week. . . . The news from the gold regions far exceeds our expectations; every man that goes to the mines picks up a fortune. I have had a lump of pure gold, weighing two pounds in my hand, just as it was dug. As ladies are very scarce, I expect to make money in the way of odd jobs, such as cooking and attending the sick. We expect to take passage on the steamship Oregon; if nothing prevents [us, we] will sail on Wednesday next. I send this by one of our party who married a short time before he left, being detained so long he must return and see his fair one. I want to hear from you, and all our friends. Remember me to them. Tell them if we succeed we shall give them a call in two years; some have made a fortune in three months. . . . Love to all and a good share to yourself. Write to [San Francisco.]

Your friend Jenny

San Francisco and Beyond

Edwin G. Waite

After a voyage of over five months—sailing from New York to Central America, crossing the Isthmus of Panama, and steaming north along the western coasts of Mexico and California—young gold seeker Edwin G. Waite finally arrived in San Francisco on August 4, 1849. Suddenly surrounded by peoples of all races and nationalities, Waite found himself somewhat overwhelmed by the hustle and bustle of the booming city, which at that time consisted largely of tents to accommodate the hoards of immigrants.

In the following selection, first published in *The Century Magazine* in 1891, Waite recounts his arrival in San Francisco, his brief two-day sojourn there, and his excursion to the gold diggings. Waite remained in California after the gold rush had faded, serving as both editor and reporter for several major newspapers. He went on to become a successful politician; after his election to two state legislative offices, he won the race for secretary of state in 1890.

Eureka! We have found it! The coast had many hours been anxiously watched through glasses to discover the Golden Gate, and there it was. Our long voyage of ninety-seven days from Panama was about over. The old brigantine, leaking at every seam, was headed for the opening between the rocky headlands, and in the bright moonlight, August 4, 1849, she slowly made her way, all sails set, into the mag-

From Edwin G. Waite, "Pioneer Mining," *The Century Magazine*, February 1891.

nificent bay of San Francisco. She rounded Clark's Point, and before dawn swung with the tide up to the spot occupied by the rear end of Montgomery block, between Montgomery and Sansome streets, now a half-mile inland from the water-front of San Francisco.

Coming Ashore at Boomtown

It was an exciting hour. We had received no news from home since our departure from New York on the 1st of March, and everybody was eager to get ashore for letters and papers. Not far away was a little shell of a building, probably sixteen feet square, erected on four posts, each resting on a hogshead [barrel] filled with stones and thus stayed in the mud. From this a plank ran to *terra firma*. The sun had not risen when we landed from our iron cockle-shell and wandered in squads through a straggling village, chiefly of tents; only a few wooden houses had yet been built, while three or four adobe structures told of Mexican occupation. Sand-dunes were plenty, and when the winds came in from the Pacific the dust made lively work, and gave us our first lessons in Californian climatology.

With the morning light the tents gave forth their sleepers, and such a motley tenantry! And such a stir! Americans in great variety of dress, natives of the islands, with a picturesque mingling of Mexicans in wide trousers and short jackets with a profusion of small globular buttons, their shock heads thrust through slits in their serapes and topped off with brown, sugar-loaf-crowned, broad-brimmed, heavy felt sombreros.

Ship-fare had given us a longing for a fancy breakfast. A restaurant sign attracted me, and I went in. The table was a bare plank against one of the walls of the tent; the plates and cups were of tin, and the meal consisted of fried beef, bread, and black coffee. The bill was three dollars.

Highlife in a Tent City

Some of the largest tents were devoted to gambling on a large scale, though the vice had not reached the magnitude

Some of the gold seekers arriving in San Francisco in 1849 were overwhelmed by the hustle and bustle of the booming city.

of succeeding years, when the El Dorado gambling-tent paid a rental of $40,000 a year, and $20,000 were staked on the turn of a card. In those early days these gambling-tents were the most attractive places in the larger towns. They were commodious, and were about the only places warmed by fires; they had well-furnished and somewhat tasteful bars, where liquors were dispensed at a dollar a glass. Tables were distributed along the sides, and in rows through the middle, at which monte, faro, vingt-et-un, roulette, lansquenet, and I do not know how many other games were played. When the whole was ablaze with lights of an evening, an occasional woman seen assisting at the games, and a band of music or singers giving forth a concourse of sweet sounds, crowds surged before the bar and around the tables, some attracted by the novelty, some to get warm, but more to try their luck.

On the River to Stockton

Our stay in San Francisco was but for a day or two. We had come to mine for gold, and though the inducements for business in the incipient city were flattering, even wages commanding eight to ten dollars a day, or a dollar an hour, we determined to push on to the mines. Glowing accounts induced us to try the southern mines, and a passage to Stockton was secured on an old tub of a schooner at the rate of three ounces of gold, or thirty-six dollars, per head. The deck was crowded with men of every nationality. The rolling hills, tawny, and flecked with green trees, bounding the bays of San Francisco, Suisun, and San Pablo, were novel and interesting. The very color of the earth, covered with wild oats or dried grass, suggested a land of gold. The sight was inspiriting. But when we reached the mouth of the San Joaquin our miseries began. This river has an extraordinarily tortuous course almost entirely through tule, or marshlands, that in 1849 produced bushels of voracious mosquitoes to the acre. I had never known the like before. It seemed as if there was a stratum of swarming insect life ten feet thick over the surface of the earth. I corded my trousers tight to my boot-legs to keep them from pulling up, donned a thick coat, though the heat was intolerable, shielded my neck and face with handkerchiefs, and put on buckskin gloves, and in that condition parboiled and smothered. In spite of all precautions our faces were much swollen with the poison of numberless bites. To escape the hot sun we took refuge below deck, and to drive away the pests a smudge was made on some sand in the bottom of the boat, which filled the hold almost to suffocation. The mosquitoes were too ravenous to be wholly foiled by smoke. I think I never endured such vexation and suffering. Sleep was impossible. The boat had to be worked by hand around the numerous bends, and half the time the sails were useless for want of wind. It was a burning calm in the midst of a swamp. But even in our distress there was a humorous side, provoking grim smiles at least.

Onward to the Mines

We finally arrived at Stockton, then also a village of tents. The newest style of architecture called for light frames on which canvas was tacked for sides and roof. There was no need of windows except for air currents, light enough coming through the cloth. We were impatient to go on to our destination, the Big Bar of the Mokelumne River, and soon were on the way with pack-mules and horses hired for the purpose. Camping on the bank of the Calaveras the first night, we were treated to our first serenade by coyotes. A peculiarity of this small wolf is that he can pipe in any key, fooling you with the belief that he has twenty companions, though one little wretch is making all the noise. We passed the plain of the San Joaquin Valley, with its dark, spreading liveoaks, like an old orchard miles in extent, and began the ascent of the foothills. Brown and red soil made its appearance hot and dusty; nut-pines were mingled with oaks and manzanitas, ceanothus, buckeye, and poison oak. Wild oats and burr clover still remained in patches unfound by the cattle of the plain. The air was dry, but grew more bracing. The trail wound among trees, around hills, through ravines, and sometimes up steep ascents, but at last, on the third day from Stockton, after a journey of more than seven thousand miles by land and sea, we reached the mines.

Crossing the Sierra Nevada

William G. Johnston

Young William G. Johnston was lucky to be a member of a select group of gold seekers who joined a wagon train bound for California in early 1849. Led by experienced guide Jim Stewart, the heavily laden expedition averaged an incredible twenty-two and a half miles per day through often poorly known wilderness, and some days covered as much as thirty-five to forty miles.

Eventually completing its two-thousand-mile trek in just under ninety days, Johnston's expedition became the first wagon train to make it to the gold country of California. In the following excerpt from his memoir *Overland to California*, Johnston describes the arduous final leg of the journey over the rugged Sierra Nevada mountain range.

Tuesday, July 17th.—The trail continued over a sandy plain, following the river, but seldom in sight of it. Our camp at noon and at night was beside it. On account of the fatiguing march of yesterday, we were late in getting started, and laid by most of the afternoon, traveling in the cool of the evening.

In the morning we obtained our first glimpse of the snowy caps of the Sierra Nevada. Distance, ten miles.

Wednesday, July 18th.—Our route still followed Carson River. A rainstorm accompanied by thunder and lightning visited us in the afternoon as we lay encamped in a grove of cottonwoods. Distance, twenty-six miles.

From William G. Johnston, *Experiences of a Forty-Niner,* first published in Pittsburgh, 1892; reprinted as *Overland to California* (Oakland, CA: Biobooks, 1948).

Approaching the Mountains

Thursday, July 19th.—Carson River, as we ascended it, began to assume more of the characteristics of a mountain torrent, dashing onward in great haste; for we had begun to lift ourselves over spurs of the mountains. And as the road became rougher, many rocks and boulders lying in our way, we found it necessary to lighten the wagons by packing portions of their contents on the backs of mules which the men had been riding. Our evening camp was close to the base of the great Sierra, its skyward precipices, black and frowning, forming barriers which neither man nor beast could attempt to scale. It was pleasant once again to be in a region abounding with pine trees, where the luxury of cheerful camp fires could be enjoyed. Distance, twenty-five miles.

Friday, July 20th.—In the early morning our course lay in a southern direction, near the base of the mountains.

A party of native Californians were met riding on mules and driving others with packs. They were about fifteen in number, and an Indian woman having a babe strapped to her back, followed them on foot. They said that they had come from Sutter's Fort, and were bound for Mary's River, where their families were encamped. Whatever truth there may have been in this statement, it is more than probable they were prospecting for gold.

Difficulties of the Ascent

In the afternoon, entering a valley between high mountains, we followed it for a time until we reached a narrow gap or cañon, where we began the ascent of the Sierras. A turbulent mountain stream spanned by a corduroy bridge was crossed. This, we learned from Mr. Sly, had been built by the Mormon battalion on its return to Salt Lake. The stream in its precipitous course dashed furiously against great rocks, which lay in its way, foaming and fretting madly; scarce more so than did we when having got over the bridge, we found the road frightfully steep, quite narrow and beset with rocks. Had not others preceded us we might have questioned whether such difficulties were not insurmountable.

Within the narrow gap which we ascended the sun never enters, and the air had the chilliness of an ice house. Our night camp at seven o'clock was made alongside the mountain torrent. Grass was scarce, and the mules were obliged to subsist on the recollection of excellent pasturage enjoyed in the morning; a fodder not very fattening. Distance, twenty-five miles.

Saturday, July 21st.—Following the course of the little mountain stream; twice crossing it, where rocks well nigh choking it, presented barriers almost impassable, we continued climbing upward. Some large trees uprooted by storms were in our way, and greatly impeded our progress; being unable to go around them, we were obliged to go over them, lifting the wheels on the side next them, for the doing of which all latent energies were pressed into service. On two occasions high above us were benches, or levels, to gain which precipitous flights of a hundred feet in one instance and about sixty in another had to be overcome. To make these ascents with loaded wagons was not thought of; it was sufficiently difficult by doubling of teams, in addition to the use of ropes, to lift the empty wagons, taking one at a time and returning for the next, and so on until all were carried up. Nor was this accomplished without the use of such

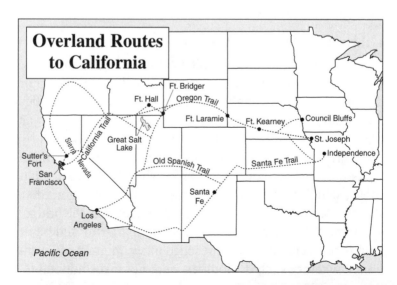

moral suasion [persuasion] as the wildest hallooing, the loudest of whip cracking, and the most extraordinary profanity that ever saluted ears, whether of dumb beasts or of men; indeed, the air seemed densely blue with oaths while all this was in progress. Then packs had to be made for the backs of the mules, for in this way the contents of the wagons were on these occasions carried upward. The amount of labor required, for what in a few sentences we have attempted to describe, was simply beyond conception. And if for a subject portraying immense muscular energy an artist stood in need, I doubt if so fine an example could be found anywhere as was here exhibited on this difficult pass of the Sierra, by those earnest, struggling toilers, the Spanish mules. With what firmness and determination their hoofs were planted; how resolutely every joint and sinew entered upon its task; while with nostrils distended and smoking, and flesh quivering in every fibre, how fearful the strain! The indications were unmistakable, that rather than not accomplish the work assigned them, they would have fallen—exhausted—lifeless in their tracks.

After surmounting the ridge up which men as well as mules toiled with such stubborn persistence, we soon began to descend, and slowly wound about until we came to a wide and beautiful valley, walled about by the everlasting mountains, whose snow-crowned summits seemed as pillars supporting the sky.

Our camp for the night was in a grove of great, wide spreading oaks, near to good pasturage and fine springs of water. Distance, twelve miles.

The Toil Continues

Sunday, July 22d.—Early in the morning a cloud of mist veiled the mountain tops, while a thick coating of frost overspread the ground, and ice was found in our water buckets.

In a short way from camp we began the ascent of one of the principal ridges of the Sierra; what may be reckoned the backbone. While there was to some extent a repetition of the experiences of the previous day, we were not as then required to unpack the wagons, the grades being less severe, and our labors were consequently lessened. At times, however, double teaming had to be resorted to; eight and in some cases ten mules were used; and very often the men were called upon to put their shoulders to the wheels, while a reserve force followed in readiness to scotch [replace] them, whenever a rest was necessary. The mules carrying packs gave considerable trouble by their endeavors to rid themselves of the burdens they bore. In these attempts they rubbed close to one another, and when a tree seemed to favor their schemes they jostled against it; while at times they prostrated themselves to the earth, and rolled to and fro, in endeavors to lighten up. If they did not succeed in freeing themselves of their packs, which was seldom if ever the case, for our experience had already enabled us to acquire the art of strapping properly, they did at least get them so shifted, that we were frequently required to do some readjusting.

A number of mishaps befell some wagons in the morning, and it was found necessary to encamp at an early hour of the afternoon to make repairs.

Underappreciated Grandeur

The fatiguing labors endured prevented us from enjoying, and almost from observing, the grand scenery of these mountains while passing over them. At times cascades of surpassing beauty were seen leaping from point to point down the precipitous sides of giant peaks, but the sights obtained were attended by circumstances which could permit of no adequate time to be given for their reproduction on the canvas of memory. At times, too, we saw under like conditions a number of lakes nestling in deep depressions, mirroring trees, rocks and clouds on their glassy surfaces, and forming pictures such as alone adorn the galleries of nature, and which art in vain essays to imitate.

Today a lake of greater dimensions than any hitherto seen was passed, and was possibly the same which at a later day was named Lake Tahoe, which has become a popular pleasure resort in midsummer for the wealthier classes of California.

In a shaded ravine we saw a body of snow apparently of great depth and solidity; constantly melting, a stream of considerable size passed from under it, and it is quite possible that in no summer can the snow entirely pass away, while through a greater part of each year it is replenished by what falls afresh.

Captain Scarborough shot a black-tailed deer which he divided around; a hind quarter fell to our lot; and once more bean soup graced our mess boards; while with our cheery guests in the prevailing jollity we forgot the severe toils of the morning. Distance, seven miles.

The Going Gets Easier

Monday, July 23d.—A succession of mountain ridges were crossed with but comparatively little difficulty. Again we passed over beds of hard packed snow, and our noon camp bordered on one of them. Sheltered from the sun, the surfaces of these masses of snow never melt; whatever of melting takes place is altogether from beneath.

A forest of gigantic trees covering the sloping side of a mountain facing towards the west, and through which our trail ran, was an unexpected surprise. In magnitude, these exceeded any we had ever seen, or indeed, heard of. This was about two years prior to the discovery of the mammoth redwood trees of Calaveras and other parts of California, now famed throughout the world as among its greatest wonders. Many of these about us were eight and ten feet in diameter, and shot upward to inconceivable heights; the measurement of which we could not approximate with any degree of certainty. On very many not a limb or a knot could be seen at a lesser altitude than from seven to one hundred feet, and to their tops they were straight without the slightest inclination. The varieties were hemlock, fir and pine. The cones of the latter were larger than ordinary pineapples.

Another deer was shot today, this time "Old" Smith was the fortunate Nimrod, and once more we had royal feasting. Distance, fifteen miles.

Reaching California

Tuesday, July 24th.—A short way from camp we realized that we no longer had mountains to climb; our route lying over the foothills at the western base of the Sierra, and through valleys lying between. In point of fact we had reached California, being within the basin drained by the Sacramento River. Early in the morning, Stewart, Sweigler and Scarborough left the train to push on by themselves to try their fortunes at gold hunting, having obtained information that some placer mines were not far distant. Whilst it was easy to foresee that in a brief time these separations would become general, we could not but feel sad at this occurrence; the first sundering of ties that in the past few months have bound us closely together. Especially was this the case in parting from our stalwart leader, Stewart, whose work in bringing us to what may be properly considered the end of our journey, has been so thoroughly accomplished. His superior judgment and never-tiring energy has stood us well in the numberless difficulties encountered. Though in his effort to place our train in the lead of all others, he met a temporary check almost at the moment of success, by reason of the misdirection given him at the South Pass of the Rocky Mountains, yet he never suffered this or any other disappointment to abate his perseverance, and now as the fruit of these untiring efforts, we today realize the greatness of our achievement, in being in the lead of the overland emigration of this memorable year—OURS BEING THE FIRST TRAIN WITH WAGONS TO ENTER CALIFORNIA!

And thus while it is contemplated by our mess and by others to move on until we reach Sutter's Fort, or some point on the Sacramento River where we can dispose of our mules and wagons, we account that the journey begun by us has practically reached its consummation, having been accomplished in eighty-eight days. Distance, sixteen miles. Total, one thousand nine hundred and seventy-four.

Chapter 3

Prospecting for Gold

Chapter Preface

The true forty-niners—those who arrived in California in 1849—found gold hunting a relatively easy chore. Miners simply stood in the shallows of small rivers and streams scooping up the sandy bottom with a flat pan. The water was then swirled around until the sand separated from small pebbles and bits of rock, which would collect along the edge of the pan. Gold nuggets and flakes would also separate and were simply removed from the debris.

Although the process was relatively uncomplicated, early miners who employed it sometimes extracted as much as $400 worth of gold per day. By late 1849, however, most streams and rivers had been worked so heavily that the gold was becoming harder and harder to find. The increasingly difficult chore was further complicated by the swelling number of would-be miners who were entering the state. It has been estimated that as many as one hundred thousand people immigrated into California between 1848 and 1852.

The collision of declining gold resources and a burgeoning mining population required new, more efficient methods of extraction. Some mining parties attacked the problem with manpower, turning up entire riverbeds, sandbars, and rock-slides with picks and shovels to get at small deposits, or "placers," of gold hidden in cracks and crevices underneath. Others resorted to elaborate contrivances, such as the cradle, or "rocker," and the sluice, or "Long Tom," to separate gold from dirt and sand.

Whatever the chosen method, the work became increasingly toilsome and frustrating as gold deposits diminished and the competition multiplied. Some miners found themselves digging month after month with little to show for their efforts—always hoping that the big strike was just around the corner. Others, unprepared for and unaccustomed to the difficult manual labor, gave up after only a day or two at the enterprise. A few literally struck it rich, but with the cost of simple necessities being so high (a pound of butter sold for as much as six dollars), the vast majority were lucky simply to pay their expenses and survive.

As the immigrant population peaked in 1852, the mining techniques employed by individuals and small groups became inefficient and were steadily replaced by more mechanized processes. Small parties of miners gave way to corporations, which employed primitive cranes to scoop out stream beds and hydraulic water hoses to blast apart entire riverbanks in search of the precious metal. Companies also began to dig tunnels higher in the foothills and mountains in search of vein deposits. These large-scale operations wrought near disaster on the environment and marked the beginning of the end of the proverbial "gold rush," that brief window of opportunity that made dreams of wealth a reality for a few adventurers who tried their luck in the gold fields of California.

An Apprenticeship in Gold Hunting

William Kelly

On January 20, 1849, Englishman William Kelly embarked by steamship from Great Britain for a tour of America. After landing in New York City, he visited many eastern cities and eventually made his way westward to St. Louis. He then joined a prospecting expedition that departed for California from Independence, Missouri, on April 16.

After a 2,043 mile journey lasting 102 days, Kelly's party reached the diggings at Weber Creek on July 26. Kelly tried his hand at prospecting in the gold region before venturing on to Sacramento, San Jose, and San Francisco. He eventually returned to his native England and published a memoir of his adventures in 1851. In the following selection, Kelly relates his first experiences hunting for gold.

When the company with which I travelled to California reached the sphere of operations, it divided into different parties, some starting for the cities to build up their fortunes, others remaining to accumulate them in the mines. Fifteen of the latter remained, in three independent parties of five each; but though our gains were distinct, we erected our quarters beside each other, selected our working locations in the same neighbourhood, and communicated candidly to one another all the information we could collect. We spent a noviciate of three days amongst the Chilians and Mexicans, looking on at their operations, and getting odd

From William Kelly, memoirs published in 1852; reprinted as *A Stroll Through the Diggings of California* (Oakland, CA: Biobooks, 1950).

lessons in the art of imparting the rotatary motion to the contents of the wash-basin, so as to surge a portion of the liquid mud over the edge at each sweep, until nothing but the gold and black sand remained; the process being, simply, after throwing aside the surface-clay or sand, to loosen the hard-packed soil with picks, scrape it with a horn scoop into a basin, then dip it until it become saturated with water, when you sink your hands into the mass, removing the stones, and in searching for them mixing all into a thick fluid. This you cause to move round quickly, some of the top escaping at each revolution; more water is occasionally taken in, until all the earthy particles are carried away; then comes the process of separating the black sand, which, being of great specific gravity, requires great care and nicety, lest some of the finer particles of gold may escape with it. But in places where it particularly abounds, and the particles of gold are small, the separation is effected by the agency of quicksilver [mercury], simply by pouring it amongst the black sand and gold dust, adding some water, and mixing it about; the quicksilver, in its great affinity for the precious metal, gathering all the particles it comes in contact with, until it becomes a little, heavy, tangible heap, devoid of its elusive character: then it is put into a buckskin bag, and the quicksilver is separated by being compressed through the pores of the leather, the slight remaining portion adhering to the gold being evaporated on a heated pan or shovel.

Gaining Proficiency

An expert hand, in anything like favourable ground, can gather and wash a panful every ten minutes; and the place that does not yield a quarter of a dollar to the panful is not considered worth working by that process, though it would give one dollar fifty cents per hour, or twelve dollars per day of eight hours' working: good wages for those who at home would have considered it a fair weekly remuneration for twelve hours' constant labour each day, but vastly too small for the large class who, "just for a lark," come out to rough it a bit, and get enough in a few months to enable them to set up as fine gentlemen for life. But places that would not pay according to the above estimate with pans can be made to yield satisfactorily with cradles, or washers as some call them, because so much larger a proportion of work can be got through with that machine, which is constructed by making a semicircular trough, say five feet long by sixteen inches in diameter, and placing on the upper end of the top a perforated iron or copper plate, eighteen inches long, the exact breadth of the trough, with a raised wooden rim of four inches, and, immediately under it, tending to the centre of the cradle, a bar or ridge about half an inch high, with another of a similar description at the extreme end, where an upright handle (if the cradle be of a large size) about four feet long is fixed, by which the motion is imparted. In smaller ones, where the number of the party is limited, the rocker sits at the end of the cradle, rocking with one hand and pouring in the water with the other on the dirt which is thrown on the plate; and as the gold and gravel are separated from the stones, and washed down, the current carries the gravel over the bars, while the gold, being of so much greater gravity, is intercepted, the lower bar arresting any that by a jolt or awkward shake may have got over the upper one.

At the end of three days we acquired sufficient expertness to set up for ourselves, in a place kindly selected by a Chilian acquaintance, and succeeded in gathering a daily average of a good ounce to each hand—rather better than half what our more experienced neighbours were making; but as our provisions were running low, I made one of a party to go to the Mill, which town takes its name from a saw-mill having been its nucleus, in the direction of which the gold was first discovered. It is situated on the southern fork of the Sacramento, about forty-five miles from the embarcadero, as the city of Sacramento is called by the miners; and being a point from which several rich and favourite diggings radiate, it is fast growing into a large and flourishing place, with a goodly proportion of stone buildings, owing to the convenience of quarries. I here got my first sample of Californian prices, in paying fifty cents for "a drink," as a small glass of bad brandy is designated, and in a like ratio for everything else. . . .

New Arrivals

On my return to camp, I found that Mr. Goodyear's caballada [group of horsemen], together with a pack-mule train, had arrived, the latter in a wretched state, and reporting, even at that early date, great sufferings on Humboldt River. By means of the cradle we augmented our daily income by half an ounce, and on one day actually divided fifty dollars per man; but this was a most unusual amount, and occurred from our meeting a peculiar shelf, where the deposit was very thick. By the end of the week another pack-mule company came in, and several fresh hands from the coast, all the latter of the amateur or dandy class of diggers, in kid gloves and patent leather boots, with flash accoutrements and fancy implements, their polished picks with mahogany handles, and shiny shovels resembling that presentation class of tools given to lords, baronets, and members of parliament, to lay a first stone, or turn the first sod on a new line of railway. It was good fun to see those "gents" nibbling at the useless soil, and then endeavouring to work their pans with outstretched hands, lest they should slobber their ducks. Subsequently I used to meet numbers of this school wending their way back to the coast from the various diggings, damning "the infernal gold," and cutting "the beastly diggings" in disgust.

Nine-tenths of the new arrivals were Americans, who resorted, as we did in the first instance, to the Chilians and Mexicans for instruction and information, which they gave them with cheerful alacrity; but as soon as Jonathan got an inkling of the system, he, with peculiar bad taste and ungenerous feeling, organised a crusade against those obliging strangers, and chased them off the creek at the pistol's mouth. Our messes were canvassed to take part in the affair, but declined becoming engaged in any such proceeding, which was likely to have led to our own expulsion: in fact, the Yankees regarded every man but a native American as an interloper, who had no right to come to California to pick up the gold of the "free and enlightened citizens."

The gold at the Weber [River] diggings was all in moderate sized particles, and of particularly fine and pure quality, less capriciously deposited than in most of the other diggings I visited, the average returns of all being tolerably uniform where equal industry was employed. All hands fixed themselves on the borders of the creek for the convenience of water; but I found the dirt (the technical name of the soil subjected to the washing ordeal) on the hillside, at a good elevation above the stream or its winter water-marks, fully

Adopting a Code

Scotsman William Downie arrived in San Francisco on June 27, 1849, but his sojourn there was brief—the gold fever had overpowered him. He soon departed for the foothills of the Sierra, and he eventually settled on the forks of the Yuba River in October. He remained there prospecting, and in the following years the town that would come to be known as Downieville grew up around him.

With no legal authority present to arbitrate claim disputes, local leaders were forced to adopt codes of conduct to regulate mining operations. On March 3, 1850, a meeting was held at Kelly's cabin to draw up such a code.

Forks of the Yuba, March 3d, 1850.
"Met, according to agreement, at Mr. Kelly's cabin. Meeting was organized by the appointment of Major Briggs, as Chairman, and C.A. Russell, as Secretary. Messrs. T. Sexton, N. Kelly and H.A. Russell, committee.

Moved and seconded that the report of the committee be accepted.

RESOLVED, First.—That ten yards be the amount of each claim, extending to the middle of the river.

Second.—That each claim be staked, and a tool, or tools, left upon it.

Third.—That five days be allowed to prepare and occupy each claim.

Fourth.—That none but native and naturalized citizens of

as rich as that along its banks. I even carried dirt in a kerchief from the very hill-tops, and got a good return from it: a proof that the gold was not altogether scattered over the country by the influence of the floods, the prevalent opinion amongst the earlier miners.

Respecting Claims

In a comparatively short time we had a large community on the creek which led to rows and altercations about boundaries. These eventuated in an arrangement, entered into by

---

the United States shall be allowed to hold claims.

Fifth.—That the word "native" shall not include the Indians of this country.

Sixth.—That companies damming the river, shall hold, each individual, a claim, and have a right to the bed of the river (below low-water mark) as far as it lies dry.

Seventh.—That claims be in conjunction with their dams.

Eighth.—That all matters of dispute be settled by referees.

Ninth.—That in case of trial for crime of any kind, there shall be ten present, besides the jury and witnesses.

Tenth.—That sea-faring men in possession of American protection, shall be allowed claims.

Eleventh.—That whoever shall not be able to show his papers, shall have a fair trial.

Twelfth.—That this code of laws be in force on and after the fourth of March.

Thirteenth.—That the upper Yuba District consist of Goodyear's Bar and all above.

Moved that this meeting adjourn to the first Sunday of next month.

MAJOR BRIGGS, President.

C.A. RUSSELL, Secretary.

O.S. SEXTON,
N. KELLY, } Committee.
H.A. RUSSELL,

William Downie, *Hunting for Gold*. Palo Alto, CA: American West, 1971. First published in 1893.

unanimous agreement, that each person should have ten feet square, which, multiplied by the number of the mess, gave the limits of the allotment in a particular location: it did not, however, debar a man from moving from one site and fixing on another; and as long as any one left his tools in the space, his claim was respected. Another branch of legislation was soon called for, to suppress a system of thieving that was fast spreading; but the code of the famous Judge Lynch was unanimously adopted, and under its oral provisions any person caught in *flagrante delicto* [in flagrant violation] was shot down without ceremony, or subjected to any other summary punishment the detector might prefer. I heard of several cases of instantaneous execution, and saw at the Weber one lad shorn of the tips of his ears, and deeply seared on the cheek with a red-hot iron, for the theft of a small coffee-tin. I never took part in any of these proceedings, nor did any of the company with which I was associated; but while disapproving of the degree of punishment, and the manner of putting it in force, I must admit that some very stringent measures were necessary to keep in check the lawless and abandoned characters who flocked to the mines. . . .

The second week in August I took leave of my companions, for the purpose of travelling over the country, visiting the different mines, and comparing their various returns, as well as looking for a solution of the phenomenon of finding gold in greater or less quantities at every elevation in the extensive region of its field. I employed one of the half-caste Californians (who make excellent *vaqueros,* herders of stock) to help me to drive my proportion of mules and horses to a rancho on the Sacramento, between our camp and the city; and on my way I struck the Weber again eight miles lower, below a cañon [canyon], where it formed a pond, or small lake, on the margin of which there were a solitary tent and a small party of three at work, amongst whom was a Cornishman, who welcomed me as a countryman, and invited me to stop a day or two; an invitation I gladly accepted as the grass was good about the little lake. In the course of the evening, Mr. Williams, the proprietor of another rancho on the Sacramento, arrived with a train of vaqueros on his way up to meet the emigrants, and either buy their stock or canvass for the grazing. He took charge of my herd there, and then gave me a receipt, saving me the trouble of going down, as I wished to visit all the mines in that district before leaving. I kept a mule for my own riding and was thus enabled to get rid of my aide after the short service of one day. Mr. Williams's charge was two dollars a month per head for pasturage, and two dollars a month for insurance, which my Cornish friend advised me to pay by all means, as horse and mule stealing was becoming most prevalent, the temptation being very great, from the enormous prices given below for animals by emigrants arriving by the Isthmus and Cape Horn routes, who could not stir without them.

Observing an Expert

I spent that evening and next day with Mr. Jones's company. He was a practised hand at the gold-digging business, and set his party to work more systematically than any other I had yet seen. They took their dirt from a steep incline considerably above the winter level of the stream, in a stratum of hard-packed, dry, bluish clay, almost as hard as rock, with a slight surface covering of earth, which yielded prodigiously, giving seventeen ounces for their day's work, nearly one hundred dollars per hand, while Jones admitted to me that on some days they divided as much as one pound each. He showed me, by washing panfuls gathered at different spots about, that the deposits were pretty general and alike, and pressed me to take up my quarters beside him, which I was not prepared to do at the time; but I wrote a note to my friends above by the returning Californian, recommending them to shift their quarters as soon and as quietly as they could: an advice they followed promptly and with great profit. . . .

I took leave of my friend Jones and my countryman Williams, and went to another digging, called the Great Cañon, lying north-east from the Weber, where I got into a chain of lofty hills, thinly wooded with fir and white oak, and steeper on the sides than I ever before saw mere clay hills, the Great Cañon lying between two parallel ranges, at a depth of several hundred feet, shaped like a wedge, and so narrow below that there was barely standing-room. The gold was all at the bottom, for the slopes were too steep to afford it a resting-place. There was a large camp of Spanish settlers adjacent when the first American diggers arrived who were said to have gathered vast quantities; but even then there was quite enough to repay hard work very liberally. From the nature of the locality, it did not admit of operations on a large scale at any one place. Four-fifths of those I saw working there were doing so individually, with pans, using most generally large bowie-knives, with which they picked the gold from the crevices of the rocks in the bed of the stream, then almost dry, and scratched the gravelly soil from amongst the roots of the overhanging trees, which was generally rich in deposits. It was one continuous string of men, single file, throughout its entire length (about four miles). All admitted they were doing well, so far as acquisition was concerned, but complained of their health and the bad air: no refreshing breeze could ever visit them at the bottom, and the labour of going up and down, morning and evening, was too great to permit of their erecting their camps above. I stopped one night in the cañon, but could not get any sleep, from the sultry suffocating effects of the confined atmosphere.

The gold at the Great Cañon ran both larger and smaller than on the Weber, and was amalgamated with large quantities of fine black sand, which the miners—most of whom were raw hands—blew off from the gold, in their anxiety to arrive at the final process. A keen old blade turned their impatience to account by shamming decrepitude, and pretending that in his weakly state, being unequal to the toil of mining, he was compelled to resort to the poor and profitless branch of gathering the black sand, which he sold as a substitute for emery. In pursuance of this trade, he went about in the evening with a large bag and a tin tray, requesting the "green 'uns" to blow their black sand on to it, and returning to his tent with his daily burden, when, by the agency of quicksilver, he secured double the average of the hardest working miner in the cañon. I saw the old lad going circuit on the evening I was there: his game had not then been discovered, though I remarked to [the doctor] with whom I stayed that I was certain he carried away large quantities of gold-dust in the sand.

Diggings on the Mokelumne River

Bayard Taylor

As a young boy growing up in Chester County, Pennsylvania, Bayard Taylor developed wanderlust and a love of writing. Although he most desired to achieve success as a poet and novelist, his talents would lead him to a career in travel writing and journalism.

He began learning his trade while working as a copy boy and typesetter for the *Village Record* in West Chester, Pennsylvania. Although he had signed on for a four-year apprenticeship, Taylor abruptly changed his plans midcourse and traveled to Europe with his brother. After publishing an account of the journey upon his return, he was offered an editorial position from Horace Greeley at the *New York Tribune.*

Soon after he joined the newspaper, the first authentic reports of the gold discoveries in California reached the East Coast. Given the sensational nature of the news, Greeley became anxious to send a journalist for firsthand reporting of the phenomenon. Taylor was the logical choice.

Taylor reached California in the summer of 1849 and began a four-month tour of the gold country. Along the way, he forwarded reports back to the *Tribune* by any means available, and he eventually returned to New York in the spring of 1850. Later that year he published his book *Eldorado*, from which the following excerpt is taken.

From Bayard Taylor, *Eldorado; or, Adventures in the Path of Empire,* household edition (New York: Putnam, 1882).

Our first move was for the river bottom, where a number of Americans, Sonorians [Mexicans], Kanakas [Native Americans], and French were at work in the hot sun. The bar, as it was called, was nothing more nor less than a level space at the junction of the river with a dry arroyo or "gulch," which winds for about eight miles among the hills. It was hard and rocky, with no loose sand except such as had lodged between the large masses of stone, which must of course be thrown aside to get at the gold. The whole space, containing about four acres, appeared to have been turned over with great labor, and all the holes slanting down between the broken strata of slate to have been explored to the bottom. No spot could appear more unpromising to the inexperienced gold-hunter. Yet the Sonorians, washing out the loose dust and dirt which they scraped up among the rocks, obtained from $10 to two ounces daily. The first party we saw had just succeeded in cutting a new channel for the shrunken waters of the Mokelumne, and were commencing operations on about twenty yards of the riverbed, which they had laid bare. They were ten in number, and their only implements were shovels, a rude cradle for the top layer of earth, and flat wooden bowls for washing out the sands. [Mr.] Baptiste took one of the bowls which was full of sand, and in five minutes showed us a dozen grains of bright gold. The company had made in the forenoon about three pounds; we watched them at their work till the evening, when three pounds more were produced, making an average of seven ounces for each man. The gold was of the purest quality and most beautiful color. When I first saw the men carrying heavy stones in the sun, standing nearly waist-deep in water, and grubbing with their hands in the gravel and clay, there seemed to me little virtue in resisting the temptation to gold-digging; but when the shining particles were poured out lavishly from a tin basin, I confess there was a sudden itching in my fingers to seize the heaviest crowbar and the biggest shovel.

A company of thirty, somewhat further down the river, had made a much larger dam, after a month's labor, and a hundred yards of the bed were clear. They commenced washing in the afternoon and obtained a very encouraging result. The next morning, however, they quarreled, as most companies do, and finally applied to Mr. James and Dr. Gillette, two of the principal operators, to settle the difficulty by having the whole bed washed out at their own expense and taking half the gold. As all the heavy work was done, the contractors expected to make a considerable sum by the operation. Many of the Americans employed Sonorians and Indians to work for them, giving them half the gold and [supplying them with] provisions. Notwithstanding the enormous prices of every article of food, these people could be kept for about a dollar daily—consequently those who hired them profited handsomely.

After we had taken the sharp edge off our curiosity, we returned to our quarters. Dr. Gillette, Mr. James, Captain Tracy, and several other of the miners entertained us with a hospitality as gratifying as it was unexpected. In the evening we sat down to a supper prepared by [Mr.] Baptiste and his partner, Mr. Fisher, which completed my astonishment at the resources of that wonderful land. There, in the rough depth of the hills, where three weeks before there was scarcely a tent, and where we expected to live on jerked beef and bread, we saw on the table green corn, green peas and beans, fresh oysters, roast turkey, fine Goshen butter, and excellent coffee. I will not pretend to say what they cost, but I began to think that the fable of Aladdin was nothing very remarkable, after all. The genie will come, and had come to many whom I saw in California; but the rubbing of the lamp—aye, there's the rub. There is nothing in the world so hard on the hands.

A Toilsome Enterprise

I slept soundly that night on the dining-table, and went down early to the river, where I found the party of ten bailing out the water which had leaked into the riverbed during the night. They were standing in the sun, and had two hours' hard work before they could begin to wash. Again the prospect looked uninviting, but when I went there again towards noon, one of them was scraping up the sand from the bed with his knife, and throwing it into a basin, the bottom of which glittered with gold.

Every knifeful brought out a quantity of grains and scales, some of which were as large as the fingernail. At last a two-ounce lump fell plump into the pan, and the diggers, now in the best possible humor, went on with their work with great alacrity. Their forenoon's digging amounted to nearly six pounds. It is only by such operations as these, through associated labor, that great profits are to be made in those districts which have been visited by the first eager horde of gold-hunters. The deposits most easily reached are soon exhausted by the crowd, and the labor required to carry on further work successfully deters single individuals from attempting it. Those who, retaining their health, return home disappointed say they have been humbugged about the gold, when in fact they have humbugged themselves about the *work*. If anyone expects to dig treasures out of the earth, in California, without severe labor, he is woefully mistaken. Of all classes of men, those who pave streets and quarry limestone are best adapted for gold-diggers.

Running the Sluices

Daniel C. Fletcher

Daniel C. Fletcher was lucky to make it to the prospecting fields of California at all. Although the gold fever had struck both him and his older brother Theodore in 1849, their father had objected to them going to California because of the many newspaper accounts reporting deaths of travelers from diseases contracted while crossing Panama.

To the consternation of his father, Theodore eventually booked passage aboard a steamer bound for Panama in early 1852. Discovering that Theodore had purchased a ticket only for himself, the father forced him to acquire another one for Daniel. If Theodore were going to go, the father reasoned, he would be safer traveling with a companion. Luckily for young Daniel, that companion turned out to be him.

The boys made it to California and settled at Grass Valley, an encampment situated about four miles outside of Nevada City in the foothills of the Sierra Nevada. After working at various odd jobs in the area, the boys took to mining in earnest. In the following excerpt from his book *Reminiscences of California and the Civil War*, Daniel describes the mining operations of the Grass Valley ravine.

The placer mines of Grass Valley extended from the surface to a depth of two hundred and twenty-five feet. Eureka slide, situated beyond the head of Grass Valley ravine, was two hundred and twenty-five feet deep. The pay dirt, or lead, of this mine was about fifty feet wide, and from six inches to two or three feet deep, and was very rich. It was a

From Daniel C. Fletcher, *Reminiscences of California and the Civil War* (Ayer, MA: Press of Huntley S. Turner, 1894).

continuation of Grass Valley slide. My brother Theodore worked drifting in Grass Valley slide a short time for one of the owners, John McCoy, who was sick, for which he received seven dollars a day. It was a wet, disagreeable place to work. Drifting consists of digging out a passage in the earth, usually between shaft and shaft, following along the lead and taking out the pay dirt.

The gold is found near the bed rock, but not below it. The pay dirt usually consists of gravel from a few inches to two or three feet in depth. In the creek and ravines, where the miners first commenced to work, the poorest dirt on top was thrown to one side. Later, when labor was not so high, all this dirt was worked through the sluice boxes.

A Run of Sluices

A sluice box is made of three boards, each twelve feet long, one foot wide and one inch thick, nailed together. The bottom board is made two inches narrower at one end, in order that the small end of one box will fit the large end of another box. A piece of board, two inches wide, is nailed on the bottom and top of the box at both ends and in the middle, to make the box strong enough to hold a man. Three or four pieces of board, an inch wide, are driven inside the big end of the box, four inches from the end, two inches apart to prevent the gold from leaving the box. A run of sluices is composed of twenty or more boxes, one after the other. The longer the run the more gold will be saved. One end of the box is raised two, three, four and sometimes six inches higher than the other end, thereby making one end of a long run several feet higher than the other. The boxes are usually on two stakes, one on each side, nailed together by a piece of board about a foot wide. The boxes must be perfectly tight, so that the water, gold and quicksilver can not get out. A piece of cotton cloth two inches wide is put around the small end of the box before it is put into the large end to prevent its leaking. If it leaks after that, it is calked with cotton cloth. The water is let into the upper box, and goes down through the whole run of boxes. The pay dirt is put into the boxes with a shovel. The water washes the dirt and gravel out. If there are any large stones that the water will not carry out of the box, a man walking on top of the boxes, throws them out with a long-handled fork.

Extracting Gold

The gold, being very heavy, settles down into the bottom of the box, and is prevented from escaping by pieces of boards fastened in the big end of the box. When the gold is taken

Mining Terms

A wave of tourism was sparked in California during and immediately following the gold rush years. In an effort to promote the state, early California historian Charles B. Turrill published his book California Notes *in 1876. Because many of the tourists were confused by the terms used in association with mining operations, Turrill devoted a whole chapter to a detailed description of mining operations. The following excerpt from that chapter identifies the classifications of mines and the many methods employed to extract gold.*

GOLD MINES IN CALIFORNIA ARE:
    Placer—gold imbedded in clay, sand, gravel.
    Quartz—metal encased in rock.
    We will in this volume treat only of the former.
PLACER MINES ARE:
    Shallow—"pay-dirt" near surface.
    Deep—"pay-dirt" over twenty feet beneath surface.
LOCATIONS OF "SHALLOW MINES."
    Beds of ravines, or gulches; shallow flats; sand bars in rivers.
LOCATIONS OF "DEEP MINES."
    Hills, deep flats.

Placer mines are also classed according to topographical position, and the methods employed in working them.

out, a small quantity of water is run down through the boxes. The pieces of board, above mentioned, are taken out, and quicksilver is sprinkled by means of a soda bottle with a cotton rag tied over the end. The amalgam is swept out of the boxes at the end of the run with a small broom into an iron pan, water is put into the pan, then the pan is shaken over a hole, and the sand and all other impurities are washed out. This process is called "panning out." The amalgam is then strained through a buckskin bag, made for that purpose. It is then put into an iron pan and put over a hot fire, where the

Topographical Classification

Hill Claims—"pay-dirt" in, or under, a hill.

Flat Claims—"pay-dirt" found on flats.

Bench Claims—"pay-dirt" found in narrow tableland on hillsides, above a river.

Gulch Claims—"pay-dirt" found in gullies destitute of water during part of the year.

Bar Claims—gold in low collections of sand, or gravel, in rivers—exposed at low water.

River-bed Claims—gold in beds of rivers—access gained by turning river from its course.

Ancient River-bed Claims—gold found in beds of rivers now extinct.

Operative Classification

Sluice Claims—worked with sluices.

Hydraulic Claims—worked by hydraulic power.

Tunnel Claims—auriferous earth taken out of tunnels and subsequently washed.

Dry Diggings—earth excavated in summer and washed in winter, when water is plentiful.

Dry Washing—fine soil blown away, leaving the gold.

Knife Claims—gold dug from crevices with knife, or spoon.

Charles B. Turrill, *California Notes*. San Francisco: E. Bosqui, 1876.

mercury is burnt off. A magnet is then used to take out any particles of iron. The gold is then boiled five or ten minutes in nitric acid, washed and dried, and is then ready to be sold. Our company at first used to hire the druggist at the village to clean the gold, but later we bought a magnet and nitric acid, and cleaned it ourselves. Most of the deep diggings were discovered after the cracks and ravines were worked out. The dirt and gravel in the cracks and ravines was a foot to five or six feet in depth, down to the bed work.

Working a Wild River

L. Dow Stephens

L. Dow Stephens was the last of five children born to descendants of Welsh immigrants who settled in New Jersey. When he was a child, the family resettled in Illinois at the western edge of civilization. Being raised on a farm, young Dow learned the trades of farming and carpentry, but the greatest adventure of his life would not necessitate those skills.

Then twenty-one years old, Stephens left the relative security of his family and farm early in 1849 to try his fortune in the gold rush. On March 28 of that year, his mining party departed for California from Galesburg, Illinois, on an overland adventure that would include Stephens's attendance at a sermon given by Mormon leader Brigham Young at the fledgling Tabernacle in Salt Lake City, Utah.

It took Stephens a full year to reach the gold hunting grounds around the Merced River in the foothills of the Sierra Nevada. Having forded many wild rivers during his journey westward, Stephens soon found himself working in one as he began his prospecting endeavor. He would soon discover just how fickle the river waters could be.

My first experience in mining was at Merced River, where I paid sixteen dollars for a shovel, eight dollars for a pick, fifty dollars for a rocker, four for a gold pan, and thirty-two dollars for a pair of boots. Everything else was in proportion, and vegetables were out of the question, as I saw

From L. Dow Stephens, *Life Sketches of a Jayhawker of '49* (San Jose, CA: Nolta Bros., 1916).

a man pay a dollar and a half for a single onion.

My success varied from day to day, for on one day I wouldn't make an ounce, and on others maybe two ounces or more. The general belief was that if the bars paid so well in gold the bed of the river ought to prove a harvest. So we formed a company to turn the river, and about twenty of us undertook the job. An Indian squaw man, Jim Savage, had told us that his Indians had waded into the river when it was low and had taken out an ounce to the bater, or wooden bowl. This was at the horse shoe bend of the river, and after much hard work we succeeded in turning the river, and where we expected to shovel gold, we found but ten or fifteen cents to the pan. We found out afterwards that this man was known as the biggest liar at the mines, and later, while in a quarrel with Major Harvey, he was shot dead. After we found out our work was all for naught we broke camp and scattered to all parts of the mines. I drifted over on the Tuolumne River, to a place called Hurts Bar, and started work at a half ounce a day. A company of twenty had been formed to turn the river, and one of the interested parties wished me to take his place, as he wanted to prospect. After three or four weeks' work I wanted to see some money, so the company called a miners meeting and voted me this man's share of the mine. I knew this would hold good, as miners laws stood preeminent to all others, but the man never came back so I was never molested. We finally turned the river and work began in earnest. The strike was rich, and we took out gold by the pound.

Rains and Floods

Our largest day's work yielded twenty-four pounds avoirdupois weight [based on sixteen ounces to a pound]; in Troy weight [based on twelve ounces to a pound] it would have amounted to thirty-two pounds at that time. Hardly a day passed but what we took out eight pounds, and we were much encouraged and worked hard. We kept three rockers running. The largest part of the work consisted in keeping the water bailed out, and around the edge of the water was a yellow streak of gold. It looked fine, and all went joyfully for about three weeks when the rains began unusually early. We had no tents, nothing but brush shanties, and the rain just poured down all night. We had to stand up around the fire with a blanket around us. This was about the twentieth of September, and the next day about two P.M. we heard a terrible roaring of water coming down the river. We hardly had time to get our tools out of the claim until the water was upon us. It seemed about fifteen feet high. There were three dams above us, and the swelling of the waters took the first when the next gave way, and so on, and by the time the water reached us it was fully fifteen feet high, and the river rose in less time than it takes to write it. We had no dam, as we had taken the water from the other side of the river and brought it over in an aqueduct to a bar where we had a chance to extend the canal. We had made the aqueduct of whip-sawed lumber and had brought it down off the mountain by hand. It was about one hundred feet long, sixteen feet wide and four feet deep, and this will show the amount of work we had put into it. When the water thundered down the river it struck the aqueduct in the middle, and it parted and went down the river like chaff before the wind. . . .

Channeling the Torrent

So far as river mining was concerned we knew the season was over, and the men began preparations to leave and go prospecting. About this time a man came along who had owned the upper dam, with fifty-five Mexicans. He proposed to work our mine with his Mexicans on shares. He proposed to throw in a wing dam, and turn one-half the river on the other side and give us one-third of all he took out. Some of the men didn't have much faith, but as he was bearing all the expense, they concluded to let him go ahead.

The usual method in building wing dams is to build two walls of rocks, an outer and an inner wall, commencing at the shore, running out half way across the river, and keeping them about two feet apart. The outer wall is made tight with canvas on the inside, and the space between the two walls is filled with sand, canvass preventing the water from washing the sand away. This makes the dam tight. In the same manner the walls are built down stream. Our company were all anxious to get away, and I was asked to stay to look after the interest of the mine. Then Jim Murrell, the man who had leased the mine, wanted me to take charge of his work, as I was going to stay anyway. But I couldn't talk Spanish fluently, so I hesitated, but finally agreed to take charge of the work for a half ounce a day. Jim stayed around for a day or two, and then he was off. In fact he was a Texan gambler, and didn't give his personal attention to any work. I didn't see anything more of him for about two weeks, and by this time I had the work well in hand, and he seemed to be much pleased with the condition of things.

I think I never had charge of a better crew of men, they worked willingly and well. Maybe it was because they hadn't had their summer's pay as yet, but however, they seemed to take an interest, and worked splendidly. The next time Jim came around I had commenced taking out gold, and it was just as rich as ever. At night I had to keep close watch for fear the gold would be stolen from before my eyes. If the gold was stolen it wasn't because I didn't keep close watch, but because they were too quick for me. Sometimes I would have many thousands of dollars on hand and only a bush shanty for protection, then I would pack it in with one of the men and take it up to Jacksonville, where there was a store and a safe to deposit it.

Dry Digging on Weaver's Creek

E. Gould Buffum

In the summer of 1846, New England Quaker E. Gould Buffum volunteered to serve as a lieutenant for the U.S. Army in the war with Mexico. He and the other members of his unit, the First New York Regiment, were sent by ship around the Horn of South America to serve as garrisons in the U.S. province of California.

As luck would have it, Buffum was already in California when gold was discovered at Sutter's Mill. When his tour of duty expired in September of 1848, Buffum set off immediately for the mines. He would spend the next six months prospecting primarily in the environs of the South Fork of the American River, where he sometimes extracted as much as $500 of gold per day.

Before his enlistment in the army, Buffum had acquired some journalism experience working for the *New York Herald*. While still in California in early 1850, he submitted the preface for a prospective book about his mining experiences to publishers in Philadelphia. Shortly after his return to the East Coast in the spring of that year, *Six Months in the Gold Mines* was published. The following selection from Buffum's book describes his first experiences prospecting on Weaver's Creek.

The day after our arrival, in anticipation of the immediate commencement of the rainy season (a time dreaded by strangers in all California, and particularly in the north-

From E. Gould Buffum, *Six Months in the Gold Mines* (Philadelphia, 1850).

ern region), we determined to build a log house, and were about to commence operations, when we received an offer for the sale of one. We examined it, and found a little box of unhewn logs, about twenty feet long by ten wide, which was offered us at the moderate price of five hundred dollars. The terms, however, were accommodating, being ten days' credit for the whole amount. With the reasonable expectation that we could pay for our house by gold-digging in less time than it would require to build one, we purchased it, and ere nightfall were duly installed in the premises. . . .

Dry Digging

The "dry diggings" of Weaver's Creek being a fair specimen of dry diggings in all parts of the mining region, a description of them will give the reader a general idea of the various diggings of the same kind in California. They are called "dry" in contradistinction to the "wet" diggings, or those lying directly on the banks of streams, and where all the gold is procured by washing. As I before said, the stream coursed between lofty tree-clad hills, broken on both sides of the river into little ravines or gorges. In these ravines most of the gold was found. The loose stones and top earth being thrown off, the gravelly clay that followed it was usually laid aside for washing, and the digging continued until the bottom rock of the ravine was reached, commonly at a depth of from one to six feet. The surface of this rock was carefully cleared off, and usually found to contain little crevices and holes, the latter in miner's parlance called "pockets," and in which the gold was found concealed, sparkling like the treasures in the cave of Monte Cristo. A careful examination of the rock being made, and every little crevice and pocket being searched with a sharp-pointed knife, gold in greater or less quantities invariably made its appearance. I shall never forget the delight with which I first struck and worked out a crevice. It was the second day after our installation in our little log hut; the first having been employed in what is called "prospecting," or searching for the most favourable place at which to commence operations. I had slung pick, shovel, and bar upon my shoulder, and trudged merrily away to a ravine about a mile from our house. Pick, shovel, and bar did their duty, and I soon had a large rock in view. Getting down into the excavation I had made, and seating myself upon the rock, I commenced a careful search for a crevice, and at last found one extending longitudinally along the rock. It appeared to be filled with a hard, bluish clay and gravel, which I took out with my knife, and there at the bottom, strewn along the whole length of the rock, was bright, yellow gold, in little pieces about the size and shape of a grain of barley. Eureka! Oh how my heart beat! I sat still and looked at it some minutes before I touched it, greedily drinking in the pleasure of gazing upon gold that was in my very grasp, and feeling a sort of independent bravado in allowing it to remain there. When my eyes were sufficiently feasted, I scooped it out with the point of my knife and an iron spoon, and placing it in my pan, ran home with it very much delighted. I weighed it, and found that my first day's labour in the mines had made me thirty-one dollars richer than I was in the morning.

Pockets of Gold

The gold, which, by some great volcanic eruption, has been scattered upon the soil over an extensive territory, by the continual rains of the winter season has been sunk into the hills, until it has reached either a hard clay which it cannot penetrate, or a rock on which it rests. The gold in the hills, by the continual rains, has been washing lower and lower, until it has reached the ravines. It has washed down the ravines until it has there reached the rock, and thence, it has washed along the bed of the ravines until it has found some little crevice in which it rests, where the water can carry it no farther. Here it gathers, and thus are formed the "pockets" and "nests" of gold, one of which presents such a glowing golden sight to the eye of the miner, and such a field for his imagination to revel in. How often, when I have struck one of these, have I fondly wished that it might reach to the centre of the earth, and be filled as it was at its mouth with pure, bright, yellow gold.

Our party's first day's labour produced one hundred and
fifty dollars, I having been the most successful of all. But we
were satisfied, although our experience had not fulfilled the
golden stories we had heard previous to our reaching the
placers. Finding the average amount of gold dug on Weaver's
Creek at that time to be about an ounce per day to a man, we
were content so long as we could keep pace with our neighbours. There is a spirit of emulation among miners which
prevents them from being ever satisfied with success whilst
others around them are more successful. We continued our
labours for a week, and found, at the end of that time, our
whole party had dug out more than a thousand dollars; and
after paying for our house, and settling between ourselves
our little private expenses, we were again on a clear track,
unencumbered by debt, and in the heart of a region where
treasures of unknown wealth were lying hidden in the earth
on which we daily trod.

Trying and Failing

William S. McCollum

When the mania of the California gold discovery began to sweep the East Coast in late 1848, William S. McCollum was already over forty years old and a well-established doctor in his local community. However, he was not immune to the lust for adventure that swelled in the hearts of young men half his age.

Among a loose association of twenty citizens of his native Lockport, New York, he departed by ship on January 28, 1849, for the prospecting grounds of California. In the short span of one year, he would travel to and from the West Coast across the Isthmus of Panama and participate in the gold rush.

Shortly after his return to New York in the spring of 1850, McCollum published a memoir of his gold rush adventures at his own expense for local distribution. In the following excerpt from *California as I Saw It*, McCollum describes the many pitfalls encountered by men of his more refined nature when they undertook the laborious work of extracting gold.

We found [in Jacksonville, California,] a colony of diggers in tents, small assortments of goods and provisions, booths, or places of refreshment; all that appertained to a central locality in the mining districts. Our tent was added to the colony, and we soon got ready to live after the fashion of our neighbors. The only thing appertaining to mining in which we were deficient, was a Rocker, and that we procured for the moderate sum of $55. We sallied out, prospecting; found squads of miners in all directions, which we took to be pretty good evidence of plenty of gold. After

From William S. McCollum, *California as I Saw It* (Buffalo: Derby & Co., 1850).

a day or two we pitched upon a spot and went to work in earnest; turned over rocks, delved and dug with pickaxe and shovel, opened a multitude of holes, tin-panned, and rocked the cradle; in fact, made a pretty faithful experiment in gold digging, and our success did not meet our expectations. Our earnings were, each of us, generally, from $3 to $6 a day; occasionally one of us would earn $12. Mr. Bradley, being an excellent house and sign painter, very rationally concluded that he could do quite as well at his trade, at San Francisco, with less of severe labor, falling in with a return train of mules, mounted one of them, and left the mines.

A One-Ounce Mule

The departure of our friend Bradley—sorry as we were to part with him—afforded us much amusement. He paid an *ounce* for the privilege of bestriding a mule that was not even a fair specimen of his unamiable race. The pack saddle, or pannier, upon which our friend Bradley was seated, was as illy adapted to equestrian uses as the half section of a good sized forest tree, hollowed out, would have been. To accommodate himself to it, his legs were thrown out to a ludicrous extent; his stirrups, loops in the ends of a good sized rope, thrown across the huge saddle. When the Spaniard—conductor and owner—gave the word to start, Bradley pulled up the halter, the mule made a plunge, and mule and rider were soon floundering upon the ground, exposed to the stampede of the whole caravan. Our friend being again in his seat, the Spaniard insisted that the mishap was all owing to the luxury of a halter, so that appendage was removed, and off went our friend Bradley upon a good round trot, his legs thrown out by his wide seat, and seeming to describe opposite extremes of longitude. There was fun and frolic glistening in the eye of my old friend and companion the Colonel when all this transpired; and our experience in the mines had not been such as to make us humorous upon slight occasions.

Col. J. and myself concluded to try it a little longer, remained, prospected and dug for about three weeks, with but indifferent success. We had fallen into the very common er-

While some miners struck it rich in California, many others failed miserably and were forced to return home.

ror that prevailed with adventurers—not as to the quantity of gold in the soil of California, but as to the amount of severe labor, under a hotter sun than we had been thoroughly inured to, to obtain it. Neither of us had been used to hard manual labor for many years, and we found that men to endure it, such as it was in the mines, must be better fitted for it than we were. Gold was not a sufficient recompense for disease and broken constitution. Where stout able bodied men, inured to out-of-door labor, by working hard eight hours in a day, might have been pretty sure of an average earning of an ounce ($16) per day. We could not by tasking ourselves even beyond the bounds of prudence, earn half that amount. And here I will remark generally, that the abundance of gold in California, has not been as much overrated, as the labor of procuring it has been underrated. At the end of five weeks from the time we entered the mining district, we sold out our most bulky mining implements, and prepared to return to San Francisco. In the trip we had not but a little more than paid our expenses. We took passage to Stockton on an ox wagon—Col. J. continuing on to San Francisco, and I remaining at Stockton for four weeks, boarding with a Frenchman at a dollar a meal. The practice of medicine was not part of my errand to California, but I did a little in that way, upon a scale of prices of course, corresponding with the expense of living. It was generally healthy; dysenteries, bilious fevers, and scurvy, prevailing, but of a mild type, yielding readily to treatment. . . .

We found pleasant companions among the miners; many intelligent, well-educated men whose society we should appreciate any where. There are few better men left behind, than a large proportion of those who have gone to California. Our leisure hours we spent in each other's tents, in rational conversation, and amusements; sometimes, having exhausted the predominating theme—gold digging and its prospects—our thoughts would wander homewards, and all that we could imagine was going on there would be thoroughly discussed; cherished names would transpire, and fond memories would call up reminiscences pleasant and refreshing. Home, and all that belongs to it, are themes whose interest increase the further we wander from them.

Chapter 4

Daily Life in Mine Country

Chapter Preface

D igging for gold was a difficult business—hard on both the body and the spirit. Many miners had to toil twelve hours a day six days a week just to find enough gold to support themselves. Such hard work required sustenance; miners needed not only tools, provisions, and food, but also amusements to distract them from their toilsome lives. As Peter J. Blodgett points out in his book *Land of Golden Dreams*, business people quickly stepped in to fill the miners' needs:

> Mining camps and towns . . . made every effort to ensure that they provided everything the miner might require. Consequently, restaurants, dry-goods stores and hardware shops shared the scene . . . with saloons, gambling halls, and brothels.

Never picking up a shovel or a pick to prospect for gold, many of these entrepreneurs became far more financially successful than the miners they catered to. Items that people took for granted in more civilized areas became like gold in themselves in the isolated mine country. A loaf of bread that had cost four cents on the East Coast might fetch as much as seventy-five cents in the camps, and eggs were sometimes as high as $1 to $3 apiece. The situation was not much better in the burgeoning cities along the California coast—with waves of immigrants flooding in, supplies of certain goods could not keep up with demand, thereby allowing businesses to gouge prices.

Some of the successful business people in gold country were women. Of the relatively small number of women inhabiting mining towns and camps, many were prostitutes. But among the other women immigrants, most of whom had arrived in the company of their husbands or relatives, some seized the opportunity to make handsome livings fulfilling the miners' needs for goods and services. In her book *They Saw the Elephant*, author JoAnn Levy describes how enterprising women took advantage of their skills:

> One woman made $18,000 just from a single Dutch oven. Women relished their first taste of economic independence. If you could wash clothes, you could make $8 a dozen. If you could cook a meal, you could sell it for $5–$10. If you could run a boarding house, you could clear $200 a week.

A few of the business people who got their starts in the gold rush went beyond mere success to realize fortune and fame. Responding to the miners' need for durable clothing, one such man began sewing pants out of canvas and selling them at his dry-goods store in 1853. The pants became very popular with the miners, and business thrived. The proprietor's name was Levi Strauss.

Impressions of a Trader

Franklin A. Buck

As immigrants poured into California in search of gold, cities and towns were forced to grow quickly to accommodate them. Outposts and mining camps sprung up seemingly overnight, leaving food, clothing, tent shelters, and tools initially high in demand, and therefore high in price. While the miners sought riches digging for gold, entrepreneurs saw an opportunity to make their wealth a different way—by filling the miners' burgeoning needs for provisions.

Young New Englander Franklin A. Buck was one such entrepreneur. When he arrived in San Francisco in August of 1849, he found the city already glutted with most of the provisions he brought to peddle. However, Buck remained optimistic, believing that the smaller towns and outposts that lay closer to the gold fields would still offer opportunities for trade. In the following selection from his collected letters to his sister, Mary Sewall Bradley, Buck describes his first impressions of San Francisco and his journey inland to Sacramento, where he would eventually find some success plying his trade.

I found things here just as I had heard with some few exceptions. The town is growing very fast. You can see it grow every night. It already contains streets and squares, several large hotels and any quantity of grog shops and gambling saloons. This is carried on with a perfect looseness,

From Franklin A. Buck, *A Yankee Trader in the Gold Rush*, edited by Katherine A. White (Cambridge, MA: Riverside Press, 1930). Reprinted by permission of Houghton Mifflin Company.

night and day. A large number of the houses and stores are merely frames covered with canvas, and as it never rains, except in the rainy season, this answers very well. . . .

The land rises up . . . into high hills back of the town. The whole country is yellow, not a green thing to be seen and not a tree. Right off the town lies the island of Yerba Buena and the shore inside sweeps around in the form of a horseshoe, making a beautiful harbor. There are lying here over 130 vessels, most of them large ships of all nations. The ship of the line Ohio, Steam Ship Mississippi and three other men of war.

High Cost of Living

The town contains over 5000 inhabitants. Business is brisk. There are thirty or forty new buildings going up. Land is higher than in New York. The most eligible rent for $500 per month and there is not one can be bought for less than $4000. The Parker House built by Bob Parker is *the* hotel. . . . It rents for $175,000 per year. Board is $25 per week. Common laborers get one dollar an hour or six per day; mechanics $16; carmen, $3 per load.

In spite of the immense quantities of goods brought here the prices of some still keep up. Tin pans are worth $5, saleratus [a leavening agent for baking] $1.00 a lb, boots and shoes and hard ware are in good demand, but, alas for our fortunes, provisions are plentiful and cheap. Flour has come from Chili and it is only worth $7. They have glutted the market and some are obliged to sell cargoes at auction to keep them from spoiling. This has ruined our prospects, for you know our cargo was wholly provisions. If we could have looked ahead and seen what to bring we could have made our fortunes. Lumber is worth $300 per thousand. We had on deck 4 houses, 14 by 28 feet, framed. They cost $147 apiece and we have sold them for $4000 *and got the dust.* I gave one dollar and a half for a tin pail to put it in.

There is plenty of gold here, no doubt of that. It is legal tender and worth $16 the oz. There is no spurious [fake gold] either. That is all humbug. You can't counterfeit it.

During the gold rush, entrepreneurs became wealthy by selling provisions to prospectors at astronomical prices.

When we landed our goods at the foot of Sacramento Street, a little ways from the water, our men washed out several grains of gold. It is found in little scales in the sand. This was right in the street. One man stuck to it all day and got five dollars.

Looking to Get Rich

The mines are on the forks of the Sacramento and San Joaquin rivers. The miners average about $16 per day but it is hard and just now hot and sickly. The cost of transportation is so great that it cost them four dollars a day to live. I have seen several of my friends who have returned from the mines, some of them with a thousand dollars, others with a great deal less. From what they have told me I have no desire to go to the diggings. I am satisfied I can make in trade. Land speculation is all the rage and men who bought lots here last winter find themselves rich. We have arrived too late to go into this.

New towns are being laid out every day. There is a large place at the head of navigation, Sacramento City. Another town at the mouth is called Benicia, the government is building a navy yard here. It is impossible to keep sailors here. They get perfectly crazy and are all off for the diggins. Sunday a boat's crew escaped from the Ohio. They fired on them but without effect. We have kept three of our men by promising to pay them off when the vessel is discharged. The Captain and myself had to take hold and work to land cargo but it's no disgrace here. The steamer got in Monday but I received no letters from her. She will sail on the first.

Finding a Place to Sell

Friday we go up the river to try the market at Sacramento City. We can't sell here at wholesale at all. At Sacramento City we can tie the brig to the bank and retail out of here, and goods are higher there. If we can rent a lot reasonably we shall put up our house and trade in that. If not, we can sell it for a great price. I think we shall come out whole with the cargo, but no more. We have to pay a pilot from here up, a distance of 150 miles, $400! Captain Cole and I are living on board. We have the cabin all to ourselves. The cook stayed by. They are all going to leave the moment she is made fast at Sacramento City. I don't blame them. Sailors are getting $200 per month to ship on the coast. The ship Greyhound is lying here offering $800 for men to take her home but can't get a man.

I wish I could send you a *lump*. I have seen some big pieces. The largest we have weighs 1½ oz, and that's nothing. I don't regret coming out at all and just as long as the gold mines last, business will be good.

A Mining Camp

Eliza W. Farnham

Eliza W. Farnham had already developed a strong will for a
woman of her day long before she set out for California.
From 1844 through 1848, she had served as a matron in the
female unit at New York's Sing Sing prison, where she gained
a reputation as a reformer. Soon after her discharge from that
post, she learned that her husband, who had journeyed to California without her, had died there.

Needing to travel to California to settle his affairs,
Farnham organized a group of single, educated women
to make the trip with her to the Golden State. In her book
*California Indoors and Out: How We Farm, Mine, and Live
Generally in the Golden State*, Farnham recounts the nerve-
racking voyage around the Horn of South America, her experiences on her husband's Santa Cruz farm, and mining life
during the gold rush. In the following excerpt, she evokes all
the senses in her detailed description of a typical mining
camp of the era.

As you approach them, the noise of the [long] toms [a
sluice to separate gold from river water] and of the
swift current rushing through the narrow artificial channels
into which it is forced, the hum of voices and the clink of
spades among the gravel, rise up from the deep chasms to
the very tops of the mountains that almost overhang them.
The great height and steepness of these border-hills on many
of the streams, make one of the grandest features of California scenery. Some of them are two, three, and four miles

From Eliza W. Farnham, *California Indoors and Out: How We Farm, Mine, and Live Generally in the Golden State* (New York: Dix, Edwards, 1856).

high, and they rise at angles varying from 45 to 60 [degrees]. You scramble down them, in the best way you can.

Descent into Camp

Sometimes you feel as if your horse were about to turn a summerset, but you push back as forcibly as possible, by way of helping him to preserve the centre of gravity, and, with an occasional halt and then a rush—a detour to the right and another to the left—a fearful looking forward, and an anxious glance backward, you finally reach the bottom, and, drawing a free breath, once more look about you, and ascertain that, deep down as you are, there have been plenty before you; that Mary Avery keeps a boarding-house for miners on your right, and that Patrick Doyle has the best of liquors and wines for your refreshment in his shanty or tent, on your left; that John Smith, honest man, is a carpenter and no swindler, as he has so often been represented to be in the wicked world you have left up yonder; that he is ready to furnish the busy community about him, indiscriminately with rockers, long toms, or coffins, [various mining devices] as their condition or convenience may require; that the National, or the United States, or the American hotel is kept in that rough one-story hut, which, as you pass, discloses dismal rents in its cotton walls and ceilings, and allures the thirsty wayfarer by a display of a bar, bristling with bottles—and that at the El Dorado or Pavilion are billiards and bowling, and, also, of course, the more spicy and earnest games in which men are wont to try their chances for fortune or ruin.

Twice, or may be thrice, as your horse loiters through the dusty street, you see a little garden spot, wherein a few cabbages, laden with dust, plead silently for water, and half a dozen rows of choked potatoes remonstrate against their hard lot. At the door of this shanty, you perhaps see a child, which looks much like the plants; for its mother cannot keep it clean, and she, perhaps, sits within, or may be by her husband's rocker in the bared bed of the river, working it while he shovels the earth. If it be at midday, the sun pours his

Remembering the Miners

In the winter of 1864–65, celebrated writer Mark Twain visited the mining area of the Sacramento Valley known as the Mother Lode. By that time, there was little evidence of the gold rush that had all but expired only a decade earlier. In the following excerpt, Twain describes the colorful characters that had filled the region.

It was a driving, vigorous, restless population in those days. It was the *only* population of the kind that the world has ever seen gathered together, and it is not likely that the world will ever see its like again. It was an assemblage of two hundred thousand young men—not simpering, dainty, kid-gloved weaklings, but stalwart, muscular, dauntless young braves, brimful of push and energy, and royally endowed with every attribute that goes to make up a peerless and magnificent manhood—the very pick and choice of the world's glorious ones. No women, no children, no gray and stooping veterans, none but erect, bright-eyed, quick-moving, strong-handed young giants— the strangest population, the finest population, the most gallant host that ever trooped down the startled solitudes of an unpeopled land. And where are they now? Scattered to the ends of the earth—or prematurely aged and decrepit—or shot or stabbed in street affrays—or dead of disappointed hopes and broken hearts—all gone, or nearly all— . . . the noblest holocaust that ever wafted its sacrificial incense heavenward. It is pitiful to think upon.

It was a splendid population—for all the slow, sleepy, sluggish-brained sloths stayed at home—you cannot build pioneers out of that sort of material. It was that population that gave to California a name for getting up astounding enterprises and rushing them through with a magnificent dash and daring and a recklessness of cost or consequences, which she bears unto this day—and when she projects a new surprise, the grave world smiles as usual, and says "Well, that is California all over."

Mark Twain, *Roughing It.* New York: Literary Classics of the United States, 1984. First published in 1872.

light and heat into this gorge so fiercely that you scorch beneath his rays, and envy the men working in the cool stream
or upon the damp gravel.

A Midday Break

The heat will soon drive them to the shade for a couple of
hours and then all will be still for the time, save the gurgling
of water and the hum of voices occasionally raised above
the drowsy noontide tone. Between two and three o'clock
the miners straggle out again, the shoveling recommences,
lazily at first, by two or three, who are soon joined by a
score or two, and the familiar sounds return. The traders and
publicans stand at their doors or lounge upon a bench just
within; your horse is brought round looking sleepy and tired,
you mount, ride through the stream, and push him up the
opposite hill with a deal of toil and dust, and when you have
gained the dry and sunny plain, wish you could again feel
around you, if only for a moment, the dampness and cool-
ness of the "Bar."

A Dandy in the Mines

James H. Carson

James H. Carson was serving as a sergeant in a western regiment of the U.S. Army when, while on furlough in 1848, he
began prospecting in the region south of the Mokelumne
River. Eventually traversing the length of the great San
Joaquin Valley, Carson discovered one particularly rich location for gold digging at a creek a few miles north of Robin-
son's Ferry on the Stanislaus River—a creek that would eventually bear his name.

In 1852, Carson recounted his adventures in what was to
be the first book published in Stockton, California—*Recollections of the California Mines*. Tragically, Carson died in
1853, shortly before his wife and daughter arrived in California to join him. The colorful and comedic writing style that
marked Carson's exposition is evident in the following
excerpt from his book.

In the tide of emigration which set into the mines in the latter part of 1848 and during '49, were to be found every
species of the human family; and amongst the other animals,
a full sized live *dandy* could be seen once in a while, with a
very delicate pick, a wash pan made to order in the States,
and a fine Bowie knife, perambulating [strolling] through the
diggings in search of "ah very rich hole, whah a gentleman
could procure an agreeable shade to work under." Of such
cases as these, the old diggers generally made play-actors,
and gave them the whole diggings for a stage on which to
perform. The dandy has always been known to go dressed

From James H. Carson, *Recollections of the California Mines* (Stockton, CA, 1852).

in the finest and most fashionable apparel—kid gloves that covered lily white hands, small walking stick, hair usually long, and soaped down until his head shines like a junk bottle, feet encased in patent leather boots, speaking a sweet little language of his own, which is faintly tinged in places with the English tongue, was never known to have done an hour's work in his life, and the oldest inhabitants never knew one of them to have a "dem cent." Such a thing as that, of course, was never made for a digger in the gold mines, although the old 'uns used to make them try it hard.

No Place for Vanity

One of this species came into a ravine on the Stanislaus in which some thirty men were at work; it was the month of June, '49, and the heat of the sun was quite oppressive in the mountains, and most of us were lying in our camps, but were aroused by the arrival of five finely dressed strangers; four of them were professional men, who, after having struggled hard for years in the Eastern States for a fortune without success, had come to California with the intention of laboring in the mines; they were good-hearted fellows and gentlemen in the true sense of the word; such as these, the old miners always instructed, aided and encouraged by every means, in their worthy undertakings. The fifth one was a dandy, who, with his soft talk and foolish questions, soon attracted the miners' attention, and his former companions (the first four mentioned) seemed to wish to get rid of him.

For the love of fun, we agreed to take him off their hands, and instruct him in the fine art of handling the pick and spade. He was first informed that he must get an axe, cut brush and build him a camp, then to take off his fine shirt and a beautiful hat which was of that pattern known as a *plug*; and a flannel shirt and straw hat offered him in exchange. To this arrangement he could not submit, but informed us that he would not undergo such "ah dem transmogrification—that he was ah gentleman—had been raised as such, and he hoped we had common understanding sufficient to appreciate his feelings; that he had stopped amongst us because he knew we were 'dem foin [fine] fellows,' and all he desired at present was to be given a rich hole, very easy to dig." Such a place was shown him as was known to consist of the hardest earth in the gulch, and where no gold had ever been found.

Quickly Disillusioned

He set to work with his little pick, which he used about as handy as a ring-tail monkey would. After working by spells for some two hours, he had thrown out about a bushel of dirt without seeing any gold. Disheartened, he threw down his tools, and came up to where some dozen of us were enjoying the rich sight of a "dandy's" first attempt at gold digging. He was in a perfect rage—swore that the gold mines were a "dem'd humbug—that Governor Mason had written positive falsehoods, for the purpose of enticing young men from their elegant homes to people this desolate region, and he deserved to be rode on a rail for his treachery."

After he had blown off a long stream of fancy indignation gas, we advised him to cool down and go to work again, and he would have better success; to this he entered a *demurrer* [objection], stating that he was a gentleman unused to such slavery; that it was impossible for him to subsist on such unpalatable food as we furnished him with; and being somewhat short of funds, he requested us to furnish him with dust sufficient to take him back to San Francisco, where he could get into business immediately. To this request, soft and gentle as it was, we told him that it was rather inconvenient for us to comply, but advised him to *hire* some men to work for him—that he could get good hands for $20 per day, who, he might rest assured, would get out each three ounces, thus giving him a fine profit. This seemed to please him well, and he set the next day as that on which his future fortunes were to commence.

A Cruel Joke

Early next morning he was to be seen making exertions to hire men to work for him, but without any apparent success, as he soon came back and informed us that the "dem'd scoundrels had had the impertinence to grossly insult him when he asked them to hiaw [hire] out." At the bottom of the gulch, off from the rest, an old mountaineer had erected his brush house; and old trappers generally have about the same regard for a dandy that he has for a skunk; and old M. was one of the oldest stamp, and was about as pleasant a companion to mankind as a grizzly bear would prove to be. To M's camp our dandy friend was directed, as being a place where he would be sure to get one good man at least. After viewing his toilet [grooming] for a moment, off he started; the whole population of the hollow was on tiptoe to know the result of his expedition. Some felt confident that old M. would make him smell the muzzle of his rifle—others that he would work for the dandy in a way that would be quite satisfactory to a man of *feeling.* But a short time elapsed before a loud yell from the vicinity of old M's camp informed us that the beauty "vat wanted to hire gold diggers" was in a tight place.

What passed at M's camp between the two, we never learned; but the yells drew nearer, until at length the dandy and old M. were seen coming at rail-road speed: M. had a brush from the side of his shanty, with which he gave the dandy a loving rap at every jump; and as far as we could see them over the hills, the same persuasive power of locomotion was being applied. Old M. returned in a short time, swearing that "that ar 'tarnal [eternal] varmint never come to his lodge without being sent thar, and if he knew the man, he would have a lock of his 'har' to remember him by." We never saw our dandy digger again, and no doubt he never stopped before San Francisco brought him up.

At the Close of Day

Leonard Kip

At the age of twenty-two, young New York native Leonard
Kip had already completed a law degree and established a
practice in Albany, New York. However, as the extraordinary
news of gold discoveries swept the eastern newspapers in late
1848, he elected to abandon his practice and take a chance at
the gold fields of California.

After arriving in San Francisco in late 1849, Kip made
his way through Sacramento and eventually reached the
diggings. He would spend only two months prospecting on
the Mokelumne River, where he experienced average success, before returning to Albany and resuming his law practice in 1850.

During his brief adventure in California, Kip sent home
sketches of his experiences for publication in the local newspaper. Upon his return, the articles were compiled and origi-
nally published as a pamphlet in 1850. In the following
excerpt from *California Sketches*, Kip relates how miners
typically spent their time after the workday ended.

L eaving all thoughts of gold digging and its prospects,
[it] is a curious sight to look around at the end of the
day and watch the different pursuits of the miners. As soon
as evening closes, all commence straggling back from the
golshes [diggings], at which they have been working during
the day. Leaving their picks in the holes, they carefully bring
back the pans, for the wash bowl is a valuable article, serving more uses than one; the least of which is the share it oc-

From Leonard Kip, *California Sketches, with Recollections of the Gold Mines*, pamphlet,
(New York, 1850).

cupies in the preparation of the different meals. It is no uncommon thing to see the same pan used for washing gold, washing clothes, mixing flour cakes, and feeding the mule.

Passing Time

The camp fires are lighted, supper prepared, and then a long evening is ahead, which must be occupied in some way. As to books there are comparatively none at the mines, and indeed they are seldom thought of, for candles being a dollar apiece, their use would be "a pursuit of knowledge under difficulties" to which few Californians are prone. But in lieu of such entertainment, the more sedate and sober miners gather around their fires, and beguile the evening with conversation, and jests and songs. Whatever is there sung has generally some reference to the home which all have left behind them. The song wherein an enterprising traveler states that California is the land for him, and announces his intention of proceeding there "with his washbowl on his knee," I never heard at the mines; but that wherein an aged negro wishes to be carried back to old Virginia, is an especial favorite. Evening after evening it was brought forward, party after party joined in the chorus, and the melody would come pealing round odd corners and from distant tents, in heartfelt strains.

There is, however, a class of miners who take little pleasure in such relaxations, and care little for songs of home; perhaps, because many of them never had any. These can invariably be known at a glance, by their long beards, red sashes, and clattering spurs. As soon as evening comes on, these men leave their tents or the trees beneath which their blankets lie, and repair to the village, there to spend the earnings of the day in maddening riot.

A Bustling Tent Town

The village, as one might call it, generally consists of two rows of stores, forming a short street between. The stores are mainly tents, before each of which extends a rustic arbor, composed of dead boughs and twigs. The effect is certainly rather pretty by candle light, for then all the impurities and dirt of the place are thrown into the shade, and the varied costumes of the occupants are softened down so as to have a somewhat picturesque effect; but in the day time, all this is lost, and the broad glare which penetrates every corner, reveals a spot which few would care to choose for their permanent residence. Within the borders of this street, the miners throng. Wines and brandy flow freely, dice are brought out and particularly monte enchains eager groups around the different tables; lotteries are in full blast; occasional fights arise; and, on all sides commences a scene of riot drunkenness and wrangling. . . .

So it is also Sunday, except that many then leave the village and go out hunting, or bet high on target shooting. But still, whatever the occupation, strong drink flows freely, and oaths and coarse songs hold a large place in the revels.

A singular misty traditionary feeling compels the miner to leave off work upon the Sabbath. He has a faint idea that it is necessary to lay aside his implements, though why, he can hardly tell. You hear one grumbling at his toil and wishing Sunday were come, that he might leave off. Tell him that nothing compels him to abandon work on the Sabbath, or to work on any other day, and he will lean on his pick, stare you in the face, think a moment, and then declare he never thought of it before. He will throw down his tools, swear that in future he will only work when he feels inclined, and then will wander off in search of kindred spirits. Still he gradually falls again into the old track. He can find more boon companions on Sunday than any other day; he must have money too to spend with them; and so he toils through the week, at the hardest work ever known, and at the beginning of the next, spends in perhaps five minutes, his whole accumulated stock of gold.

Such a man seldom thinks upon the future. If, in the midst of his rioting, he lays aside a few pieces [of gold] for the purchase of a new shirt or a small bag of flour, he looks with complacency upon his own extraordinary providence. As long as he has the slightest, meanest stock of clothing, and a little coarse food, he is contented. He considers the mines an inexhaustible store, which, if not very yielding, will at least manage to support him, and he resolves to pass his life there—a merry, if a short one. The consequence is that some day, dysentery or scurvy, the two curses of the mines, attacks him. He has no money left to pay the doctors, and they will scarcely render him the best attention, without the usual ounce fee. The friends upon whom he has spent his money miss him at their revels, but hardly enquire about him; for one of the great characteristics of the mines is a dreadful, heartless selfishness, which seems to attach itself to the souls of all. He dies unnoticed in his tent. Perhaps a week afterwards, some one comes to borrow a tool, and for the first time, sees the dead body. A friend is called in, the two bury the corpse where it lies, and divide the tent and provisions for their trouble, and that is the end of the poor miner. It is a sad death which often is the fate of more worthy and economical persons, who, coming unknown into the mines, fall sick before saving up enough gold with which to purchase proper attentions.

Fickle Weather

Jean-Nicolas Perlot

> Young Belgian Jean-Nicolas Perlot had been working for three years in Paris as a draper's assistant when, in the fall of 1848, news of the gold discovery in California was first reported in France. The discovery was initially met with skepticism, but when the French government corroborated the story and news reports increased in 1849, Parisians went wild with excitement.
>
> Like many of his fellow citizens, Perlot viewed the prospect of striking it rich as a welcome alternative to the depressed Paris economy of the era. In the fall of 1850, he joined a French mining operation called La Fortune and set sail for California. After their arrival in Monterey on April 7, 1851, Perlot and nine of his shipmates formed a small company and set out for the southern mines.
>
> Being unaccustomed to the local climate, geography, flora, and fauna, Perlot's party struggled just to survive, much less to find success digging for gold. As the fall of 1851 approached, Perlot found his party dwindling and the weather increasingly uncooperative. In the following viewpoint from his memoir *Gold Seeker: Adventures of a Belgian Argonaut During the Gold Rush Years*, Perlot describes how he and his various companions grappled with the unfamiliar winter elements of mine country.

It was the end of September and the rainy season was about to begin. During the five months that we had been on the placers, we had not seen a cloud in the sky; but as soon as the rain began, it would fall for five or six months. People stopped working because of the lack of water; when the rivers filled, it would become impossible to start working again because of the abundance of water. The season therefore was ended; those who employed workers released them; most of the miners were preparing to return to Stockton or San Francisco to spend the rainy season there and to return to the placers in the month of February or March. They were afraid, besides, that the same thing would happen to them as to those unfortunates who, the winter before, when surprised by the rains and lacking provisions, had died of hunger and hardship while trying, but too late, to return to the coast.

A Brave Few Remain

A certain number, however, appeared disposed to remain; they alleged that winters like that of the preceding year, when it had rained without stopping for three months, were the exception, continual rains lasting ordinarily four weeks; and then, last winter, after the rain, the snow had fallen abundantly and, according to the statements of the Indians, that occurrence was extremely unusual. If then, one were provided with supplies for only three months, one need not fear famine, and one could profit from the interruptions in the rain to dig for gold. In the meantime, the merchants, not knowing whether the placers would be completely deserted, put in hardly any supplies.

Whatever the case might be, we decided, Béranger and I, that we would stay, would buy canvas to make a tent, and would provide ourselves with supplies for three months; when winter came, we would wait under our tent for the return of spring; that, in the interval, however little or much we could work, we would only be better off and more ready the following year. It would cost less, in any case, than to cover sixty leagues on foot, live three or four months in a hotel, and afterward make the same trip again. The only danger to fear was the return of the Indians, whom the snow would drive from the mountains and who, they said, com-

ing down as far as Mariposa and even farther, would kill and
steal every time they had a chance. But after all, Mariposa
already numbered eighty to ninety houses or tents; if at least
two or three persons remained in each dwelling, we would
be strong enough to resist the Indians.

This resolution taken, and abandoned claims being numerous, we settled on the almost dry river, a mile below
Mariposa, in order to work there while waiting for the water coming from the rains to drive us from the river.

In consequence of the departure of most of the miners,
the water, being used less, had become a little less scarce
and much clearer, and as it was more abundant and cleaner
in the morning, we began the day by washing the gravel extracted the day before, which took us three hours, and the
rest of the day we spent digging the dirt which we would
have to wash the next morning. We managed, by proceeding this way, to make from seven to eight dollars each per
day. We passed our Sundays in sewing the canvas of our tent
so that we would not be caught unprepared when the bad
weather began.

The Dry Season

There came a time when the water was completely lacking; the season was ended. While waiting for the rain, I occupied myself with hunting; there was found in the environs an abundance of game of all kinds, hare, rabbits,
wildcats, partridges, quail, wild geese, without counting
the bear and the mountain lion. These last two, who little
liked noise and disturbance, were beginning to stay away
from the placers, but they would return when the flats had
become peaceful again and when snow covered the mountains where they had withdrawn.

I bought a double-barreled shotgun, a six-shot revolver,
five livres of powder and twenty livres of balls and small
shot. We left in the morning, carrying on our backs the supplies for the day, one armed, the other bearing the miner's
tools. At the same time we were hunting, we were exploring
the country on this side and that, gathering observations,

sometimes making assays, with the next campaign in view. Where were we going to establish ourselves? was a question which we wanted to settle before the coming of winter. . . .

Allies Arrive

Meanwhile, we met with three shipboard companions, two of whom were members of the former company of La Fortune, in search like us of winter quarters; they were Huguet, Gaillot and Brillet. They were among those who, after our debarkation at Monterey, had become cultivators of the soil and had taken service with different farmers. But, since the month of July, they had left agriculture there and taken the road to the placers. They had even better reasons than we for not going to spend the winter in one of the coast cities where they would have had to live on their savings.

As much as we, moreover, they counted on profiting from the breaks in the rain to get a little gold. The two companies were reunited. After having tried a claim whose situation seemed promising, but where we found little gold, we resolved to settle on the claim I had had to abandon for lack of water in the month of September, and which was situated down the creek from the camp of Agua Fria and about halfway between this latter camp and the confluence of the Agua Fria with the Mariposa. Our three new companions set up their tent there too. . . . So we formed a little camp.

A Torrent Unleashed

We had laid in supplies for two or three months. The placers being more and more depopulated, the bakers and butchers had had to shut up shop for lack of clients; however, the other business houses were still going. We worked every day, a matter of killing time, for we made nothing much because of the dryness. Three weeks after our installation, the rain began and we then saw how it rains in California. It fell at first in torrents for about twenty days, without stopping for as much as two hours a day. With that, there was a south wind strong enough to break a bull's horns, so much so that one fine day, or rather, in the middle of a frightful night, the three tents were lifted at once and thrown in a tangle into the branches of an oak growing more than a hundred paces away. Lord knows how we passed the rest of that night! When day came, we divided among ourselves the rags still hanging from the tree, and we began to construct a house of dirt and wood, although it was rare in this neighborhood; only the roof was of canvas. We finished it in spite of the rain; but that took us three days, although there were seven of us. Then only could we dry ourselves, us and our provisions; but they were lost anyway: they went moldy in a short time.

Some days later, the rain stopped; but the rivers and creeks ran full to the banks and it was only at the end of eight or ten days that we were able to go back to work. We made from five to six dollars each, but the work was difficult because of the water which flooded the trenches. While working the claim, we went up the river; as we took the precaution to throw nothing behind us, the worked ground, at the end of some weeks, served us as a drainage ditch and permitted us to work more comfortably; but shortly after, the rain began again more heavily, and the overflowing river came, alas, to fill up everything. When the rain stopped again, there remained no trace of the ditch; we had to begin all over as if on virgin ground. We set to work without being discouraged, and so arrived at the extreme limit of our claim.

We had to look for another.

Fickle Fortune

But the rivers and creeks, full of water, made prospecting difficult. The Mariposa, which had become a veritable torrent, had leveled everything on the flats, and of the former diggings nothing remained. So it happened that after having painfully dug a trench on an apparently virgin claim, one discovered that one was working a vein already exhausted.

To remedy as much as possible the inconveniences of this situation, the miners remaining in Mariposa were in favor of modifying California legislation as it concerned the extent of claims. Naturally they modified it to suit their convenience. They enacted that each miner had the right thenceforth not to twenty-five but to one hundred and fifty feet of land along and on both banks of no matter what river or creek. Only, when the width of the watercourse exceeded eight yards, the claim was reduced by half in the sense that it could extend on only one bank. The claim without watercourse remained twenty-five feet. The result was that the exploitation on a grand scale of mining lands became possible. Companies were formed, claiming great extents of land along the rivers and creeks; during the winter they carried out preparatory works for the next campaign. At these works were employed a certain number of laborers recruited among the new arrivals, who, in spite of the season, continued to increase almost as in the autumn. Since, at that time, we were not working, Béranger left me and went to work by the day for one of these companies; he earned four dollars a day. I bought back from him his share of the provisions we had left; then I found myself alone.

A Lady Tries Her Hand

Dame Shirley

> Schoolteacher Louise Clappe, affectionately known as "Dame
> Shirley," left her native New Jersey with her physician hus-
> band in 1849 for the promise of a better life in California. The
> couple initially settled in San Francisco, but Dr. Clappe found
> the overcast, damp weather there intolerable. In 1851 they
> moved to the mining country around the North Fork of the
> Feather River, where Dr. Clappe found the atmosphere more
> to his liking.
>
> During the couple's thirteen-month stay in the mining
> region, Dame Shirley sent twenty-three letters home to her
> sister Molly. The letters, later collected and published in the
> California monthly magazine *The Pioneer*, captured the
> unique perspective of a cultured woman who suddenly found
> herself living in a log cabin in a rugged environment. In the
> following letter, penned on November 25, 1851, Dame
> Shirley somewhat comically describes how her illusions were
> shattered during her first attempt at prospecting for gold.

Nothing of importance has happened since I last wrote
you, except that I have become a *mineress*; that is, if
having washed a pan of dirt with my own hands, and procured therefrom three dollars and twenty-five cents in gold
dust, (which I shall inclose in this letter), will entitle me to
the name. I can truly say, with the blacksmith's apprentice
at the close of his first day's work at the anvil, that "I am

From Dame Shirley, *The Shirley Letters* (San Francisco: T.C. Russell, 1922).

sorry I learned the trade"; for I wet my feet, tore my dress, spoilt a pair of new gloves, nearly froze my fingers, got an awful headache, took cold and lost a valuable breastpin, in this my labor of love. After such melancholy self-sacrifice on my part, I trust you will duly prize my gift. I can assure you, that it is the last golden handiwork you will ever receive from "Dame Shirley."

Pleasure Parties

Apropos, of lady gold-washers in general,—it is a common habit with people residing in towns in the vicinity of the "Diggings," to make up pleasure parties to those places. Each woman of the company will exhibit on her return, at least twenty dollars of the *oro* [gold], which she will gravely inform you she has just "panned out" from a single basinful of the soil. This, of course, gives strangers a very erroneous idea of the average richness of auriferous [gold-bearing] dirt. I myself thought, (now don't laugh,) that one had but to saunter gracefully along romantic streamlets, on sunny afternoons, with a parasol and white kid gloves, perhaps, and to stop now and then to admire the scenery, and carelessly rinse out a small panful of yellow sand, (without detriment to the white kids, however, so easy did I fancy the whole process to be), in order to fill one's workbag with the most beautiful and rare specimens of the precious mineral. Since I have been here, I have discovered my mistake, and also the secret of the brilliant success of former gold-washeresses.

False Treasures

The miners are in the habit of flattering the vanity of their fair visitors, by scattering a handful of "salt" (which, strange to say, is *exactly* the color of gold dust, and has the remarkable property of often bringing to light very curious lumps of the ore) through the dirt before the dainty fingers touch it; and the dear creatures go home with their treasures, firmly believing that mining is the prettiest pastime in the world.

I had no idea of permitting such a costly joke to be played upon me; so I said but little of my desire to "go through the motions" of gold washing, until one day, when, as I passed a deep hole in which several men were at work, my companion requested the owner to fill a small pan, which I had in my hand, with dirt from the bedrock. This request was, of course, granted, and, the treasure having been conveyed to the edge of the river, I succeeded, after much awkward maneuvering on my own part, and considerable assistance from friend H., an experienced miner, in gathering together the above specified sum [$3.25]. All the diggers of our acquaintance say that it is an excellent "prospect," even to come from the bedrock, where, naturally, the richest dirt is found. To be sure, there are now and then "lucky strikes"; such, for instance, as that mentioned in a former letter, where a person took out of a single basinful of soil, two hundred and fifty-six dollars. But such luck is as rare as the winning of a hundred thousand dollar prize in a lottery. We are acquainted with many here whose gains have *never* amounted to much more than "wages"; that is, from six to eight dollars a day. And a "claim" which yields a man a steady income of ten dollars *per diem,* is considered as very valuable.

A Miner's Sunday

Prentice Mulford

New York native Prentice Mulford was only fourteen years of age when the first reports of the gold discoveries began to appear in the eastern newspapers in 1848. He was too young then to follow his dream of traveling to California, but he eventually made his way to San Francisco via clipper ship in 1856.

The gold rush was already fading by the time Mulford reached the mines of Tuolomne County, but he nevertheless realized his dream of prospecting for gold. During his sixteen-year residence in California and subsequent travels in Europe, Mulford recorded stories and developed writing skills that would lead him to success as a lecturer, essayist, and columnist upon his return to the East Coast.

Toward the end of his life, Mulford collected his writings in a memoir titled *Life by Land and Sea.* In the following selection from his book, he eloquently recalls how a typical miner's Sunday was spent during the gold rush years.

The Sunday sun . . . streams through the cabin window and through the chinks of the cabin wall. It is the same sunshine as that of the week day. Yet as the miner wakes and realizes it is Sunday, it has a different appearance and conveys a different impression from that of the weekday sun. Everything seems more quiet, more restful, and even more staid and serious. There belongs to it and to the landscape as he looks out a flavor of far-away Eastern Sabbath bells and Sunday morning's hush and longer family prayer than usual and Sunday-school. But there is not a church bell

From Prentice Mulford, *Life by Land and Sea* (New York: Needham, 1889).

within ten miles and there never will be one heard on this flat. There is not the least approach to church society or religious organization or observance. There is not, so far as known, so much as a man in the least religiously inclined. We are a hard lot. No work on the claim to-day. The pick and shovel will rest where thrown Saturday afternoon and only a trickle of yellowish water from the reservoir will seep through the long line of sluices instead of yesterday's muddy surge rushing through—sand, gravel and grating pebble and boulder.

Cleaning Up for Camp

But there is work of another sort to be done and a great deal of it. After breakfast [comes] shaving. That small mirror of most imperfect glass, whose reflection distorts the features, screwing up one side of the face and enlarging the other in an unnatural fashion, is suitably adjusted. A smell of soap pervades the air. He lathers and shaves and relathers and reshaves with a tedious and painful precision, the while making faces at himself in the glass as he brings one portion of his countenance after another more directly under the sweep of the razor. In some cases he comes off with a few scratches or leaves a hirsute oasis here and there of uncut bristle. Black pantaloons, a white shirt, a felt or straw hat, a linen duster and the Sunday boots—this is his dandy outfit. In his pocket is a buckskin purse, once yellow, now faded to a dull gray, holding gold dust, a few ounces more or less, perhaps five, perhaps ten. It is the company dust and is to be sold and turned into bright, yellow gold pieces. And why all this preparation? To go to camp. Camp is three miles away over the mountain yonder. A group of ramshackle cabins, alternating with saloons, three grocery stores, a hotel, an express office and a Justice of the Peace, all in a hot gulch, with hillsides long ago swept of trees, scarred with cuts and streaked with patches of dry yellowish ledge. "Camp" to him has all the importance and interest of a great metropolis. It is the centre of news. The stage passes through it on the way to a larger camp. Two boss gamblers reside there. There is a faro game on occasions, a billiard table with a mountainous sort of bed, where the balls roll as they please and after an eccentric fashion of their own.

The camp is for him the first nerve-centre of civilization and the only outlet to the great world which he has left. You, fresh from the great city, regard this dilapidated place as an out-of-the-way corner; but to him, living on his remote flat, with but two cabins in sight for as many miles, camp is a place of importance. The news is fresh here; the city papers are here; the political candidates speak here; the one-horse show comes here and all the minor lawsuits are tried here. Camp is reached after a long, hot walk. He suffers in his store clothes from the heat. In his working every-day flannels he would not so much mind it, but the restraint and chokiness of starched linen are fatiguing. It is laborious even to be "dressed up" on a hot day. Of this he is not aware. He has not yet so far analyzed into the depth and causes of sensations, yet it is a labor in tropical weather to wear and bear good clothes—clothes which cannot safely be perspired in; clothes which one can't "lop down" in; clothes which require care in the keeping, as well as dignity and uprightness; I mean physical uprightness. He never so much suffered from the heat on a week day as on Sundays and the cause was mainly the difference between clothes which demanded consideration and respect and those which did not.

Gathering at the Bar

He repairs first to the Magnolia. He has long in imagination seen it from afar. How cool is the big barroom. The landlord keeps the floor well wet down. That Magnolia floor is one of the few places where water, unmixed with other fluid, is useful and grateful. How comforting and soothing is the first drink. A long drink in a long tumbler, with plenty of ice, soda water and whiskey. If heaven be anywhere as a material locality it is in that first cool drink after a three-mile July tramp over the kiln-dried hills and herbage of the California foothills. The Magnolia is the social heart-centre of camp. There he finds the doctor. The doctor drinks with him. The doctor drinks with everybody. There, too, is the Justice of the Peace. The Justice drinks with him. The Justice holds his Court at the Magnolia. The proprietor of the Magnolia is the camp constable and between drinks during trials calls . . . the witnesses in the case. The Judge drinks with him. The Judge generally drinks. The principal camp gambler is at the Magnolia. He takes a light drink. He is a wise man and knows the advantage and profit of keeping a cool head. The regular camp drunkard sits in the rear in one of the armchairs back of the billiard table. He looks so humble, so respectful—and so dry, that our miner's heart moves to pity and he "asks him up." He complies, but not with undue haste. . . . The camp drunkard had not then so "lost his grip" as to be unmindful of a certain slowness, deliberation and dignity befitting a gentleman. But when he does arrive at the bar he takes a "four-fingered" drink.

They stand in a row at the bar. The barkeeper is mixing the "long" and the short drinks. Each man waits, says nothing and eyes every motion of the bartender. The silence is impressive. All is ready. Each glass is grasped and raised, and then from each to each, and more than all, from all to the drink donor, there is a nod, that incantatory phrase is uttered, "Well, here's luck," and the poison is down. As it rasps, they call "Ahem!" with varied degrees of modulation. But this is a careful and prudent miner and he now repairs to the store. There his dust is weighed, sold, and the week's provision ordered. His combined partners' "divvys" are put aside in a lump and safely stored. Now the weight is off his mind. He returns to the attractions of camp.

Local Gossip Is Big News

These are not numerous. There is the Magnolia, the Bella Union, the Court Exchange, the post and express office. There are the "boys." He learns the news of the county or district. The Mount Vernon is paying four dollars per day. Long Shortman has gone on another spree and hasn't done any work for the last ten days. Jimmy McNeil has sent for his wife's sister. She is unmarried. Sullivan has had another row with his wife and she has complained to the authorities. Sam Gedney is going to run for County Clerk on the Democratic ticket. Bob Delmame lost $200 at the game the other night. A San Francisco company have bought the Crazy Gulch quartz lead and will put a ten-stamp mill on it. The school-master was drunk last Friday night. Ford shot at McGillis the other night, but did not hit him. There is scandal and talk concerning the Frenchwoman who keeps the peanut stand and the Justice of the Peace. The Wiley girls, two sisters who have recently moved into camp, are making a sensation, and their small parlor at times won't hold the crowd of semi-bald and unconsciously middle-aged miners and others who are calling on them with possible matrimony in prospective. They may pass along the street about the middle of the afternoon and such "ragging out" was never seen before in this camp. The curious have investigated the tracks made by their little gaiters in the red dust of the upper road and report them the smallest feet ever seen in this section. Billy Devins of the Blue-jay claim is thought to have the best show with the eldest, and Goldberry of the livery stable with the youngest. No. He won't let his best horse and buggy to anybody now and takes her out riding three times a week. But they're snappy and uncertain, and nobody can count on them for a certainty. So runs the week's news, which he picks up with sundry drinks.

The Day Closes Quietly

He enjoys the luxury of a hotel dinner—a dinner he is not obliged to prepare with his own hands—a decidedly plain dinner in metropolitan estimation, but to him, commencing with soup and ending with pie, a sumptuous repast. It is moonlight and he takes his way back by the old trail home. Old not in years, but in association. It is but the track of twenty years or so, yet for him how old is it in thought. How many, many times he has travelled over it.

Chapter 5

The Wild and Lawless Frontier

Chapter Preface

As the gold rush enveloped California and immigrants continued to pour in, mining camps and towns were forced to grow rapidly to accommodate the miners. The law of supply and demand ensured that enterprising businessmen would step in to provide the essentials: food, housing, clothing, and tools. Establishing police authority, government administration, and infrastructure, however, was a far more difficult task. Consequently, boomtowns were often wild and lawless places where all manner of behavior was tolerated. In his book *The World Rushed In*, author and historian J.S. Holliday writes of the inhabitants:

> There were no "hometown eyes" watching them—no mothers, fathers, uncles, in-laws, preachers, teachers, neighbors. There is the freedom of anonymity. If you are anonymous, you can dare to behave in a way that you would never behave under the supervision of home—and all the weightliness that home puts upon you.

Gaming halls, saloons, and houses of prostitution sprang up to serve the entertainment needs of the miners. Some men simply desired diversion from the relentless digging, while others who had suffered disappointment and failure at prospecting took to drinking and gambling to ease their frustrations. Holliday writes:

> Thousands of young men who'd never thought of gambling turned out of desperation to make on the turn of a card what the turn of 1000 shovels full hadn't produced. To make enough to justify finally being able to say, "I can go home."

Many who came to California with the dreams of riches eventually found themselves far from home with little to show for their efforts. Debtors and drunks abounded, and those who were unable to collect themselves often turned to crime out of desperation. In a frontier land where prospectors wandered the countryside with gold nuggets in their pockets, criminal behavior was bound to flourish.

Because legal authority was usually unavailable in the remote camps and towns, local leaders were often forced to adjudicate alleged misdeeds. In the absence of deliberate leadership, mob rule often resulted. Vigilante justice was frequently swift and brutal, with punishments more often than not devised by the whims of a crowd, not the deliberations of a jury. Hanging became so commonplace that it was popularly referred to as "Judge Lynch."

The Gamblers

James H. Carson

When prospectors began to establish camps and visit towns for supplies, enterprising gamesters set up all manner of gambling operations. Seeking amusement and diversion from the toils of prospecting, many miners succumbed to the temptation. Some miners who had struck it rich in the gold fields would lose it all at the gambling tables.

In the following excerpt from his book *Recollections of the California Mines*, noted essayist and anecdotist James H. Carson provides a vivid description of gambling life in the mine country.

We who have come from the *second* families in Virginia, have been taught to look on gamblers, and those who follow it as a profession, as little superior to the devil himself. This view of the members of the *black art* may be good and just in other lands, but it is not applicable to California. To say gaming of any kind is not an evil of the most to be dreaded description, would be to argue against common sense, and all laws of morality. It is an evil—in California has become a necessary one. It is, here, sanctioned by law, and its professors constitute a large proportion of the first class of California society, and one-fourth of the entire population of the state gamble to a less or greater extent. Take the gamblers, that is those who follow it as a profession here, and they constitute a body of men of noble disposition, free, open hearted, and generous; and some of the best improvements in the state have been made by the gam-

From James H. Carson, *Recollections of the California Mines* (Stockton, CA, 1852).

blers from the proceeds of many a fool's money. The state also receives a large revenue from the license imposed on gaming. To prevent gambling, by making laws for its suppression in California, would be as useless as it would be to stand in the Golden Gate and undertake to keep out the tide with a pitch-fork. What a field for the study of human nature is a gambling house!—where the tenderest strings of a man's nature are played upon, where the pre-eminent *and* prevailing dispositions, and the hankerings of the heart for gold, become the master passion.

As the first steamer brought the first cargo of foreign masters in the "mystic art," their annunciatory proceedings in California may serve to illustrate scenes in a gambling house during the winter of '48 and spring of 1849. Previous to this arrival, "monte" was the universal game, in the cities and mines, interspersed at times with "lump o' gold" poker. In the mines, especially in the Stanislaus region, in 1848, I have seen the Spaniards, men and women, betting freely pounds of gold dust on a card, and smoking cigaritos until it won or lost, with as much indifference as if it had been so much gravel. In the coast cities, (San Francisco in particular), millions of dollars were daily staked on monte, during that winter. The scenes of these places of *amusements* have been shifted and a new set of men have come on since then.

A Typical Gambling House

It required large capital to become a monte banker, as a small concern would be *tapped* by almost any rough looking *hombre* you would meet, during that golden reign. Large banks had their crowds day and night, at which some rich scenes were to be witnessed. One-half the betters were men who, a few months previous, would have considered their characters ruined forever if they had been seen in such places, [but] were now to be seen "pungling her down," with their heads presenting a mass of hair and beard that would vie with that of Nebucadnazzar's on his return from his country sojourn spoken of by Daniel, and around which fell in graceful folds portions of the brims of hard worn "old tiles" from under which the only thing human to be seen was the end of a "jolly red nose" and a pair of eyes sticking out like a boiled crabb; Greasers wrapped in the *inhabited* folds of the everlasting *serape,* only watching for a "sure thing," on which to pile down a few pounds of the "oro"[gold]. The rather trim appearance of a few business men could also be seen mixed with the crowd of betters provided the bank was a "good thing"; jolly sons of old Neptune, who had adopted a country life in California for convenience sake, could be heard cursing a losing card; and occasionally a bag of dust would be passed in by a son of Africa, who acted as an outsider. A good house would have four or five of these tables in full operation in it at once, each with its crowd of devotees. A bar the whole length of the establishment was the next prominent feature, where "old red-eye" was, under his different names, issued in a perfect stream to thirsty suckers at fifty cents per glass. Collected in the corners were small parties, who only loved to gamble so far as to play "old sledge" for the liquors, until

Gamblers established gaming halls in the mining camps, looking to take advantage of the prospectors' hard work.

from their winnings they became so essentially "corned" as to make a hard plank or the ground, when they retired to rest, appear "soft as downy pillows are." Groups collected around old *topers* to hear them sing songs. A pair of dirty lumps of mortality, who had met after a long absence, commenced *wetting* the ties of "Old Acquaintance," until they had become so loving as to hug and kiss each other. . . . A few overpowered by the *fatigues* of the place piled up in a corner completed this faint picture of a California gambling house in '48.

Professional Gamblers Take Over

During the reign of this state of affairs, the *professors* before mentioned made their appearance from the decks of [the ship] "California." The billiard rooms in Monterey were the stages on which they made their *debut* into El Dorado. That quaint old place which had seen many a little old fashioned monte bank give way before the power of long bags of dust was made to resound with a voice which told us plainly that old things must change. These gents brought new games; the billiard tables were stripped of their cloths, and converted into tables for the different games, and stands for those who wanted to auction off extra clothing, guns, pistols, and the most approved Bowie knives. Monte, roulette, faro, ABC, twenty-one, and the sweat cloth had their representatives, who (a new fashion at the time), praised their different *ounce catchers* up in something after this style: "Here, gentlemen, is the monte bank that will stand you a 'rip'; walk up, you chaps with the long bags o' dust; jest bet what you please—it'll all be paid; pungle 'er down, punglee!" "Here, you goodhearted fellows, is the man 'vid de weel'—brought this 'ere fixens all the way from home jest to give you something to amuse you; this, genteels, is vat you calls roulette, the only game vat pays twenty-six times for one; you can just bet where you please—on any number, column, red or black side, or on the eagle bird; walk up, gentlemen, and make your bets—if you think I would cheat, why you can jest turn the wheel and roll the ball yourselves." Twenty-one would have its devotee using his powers to increase the size of his circle of betters. Faro would be extoled for its age and respectability, and the only fair game in the house, the dealer having no earthly advantage but the *splits*.

Working the Crowd

The man having the sweat-cloth being a genius of the society whose members are known as "one of 'em," held a crowd around him; he was one of the comic characters we see at times, who come on the stage in this great drama of life and divert the lookers-on for a season, and then pass off. The inside of the house being full, he had to establish himself under the portico in front. The rainy season was not over, and the gentle showers which we see falling here at times were descending in soaking torrents. In order to allow his betters a fair chance, he was standing outside directly under the droppings of the eaves that were running in perfect streams over his tarpaulin hat and India rubber coat. His cloth was spread on a bench in front of him under shelter, to which he called the attention of the outsiders by slapping his sides and imitating the crowing of a cock; and in imitation of scenes in other lands, he would, with comic gestures and a stentorian voice, cry "oysters! fresh clams! hot corn!" and many other kinds of commodities that California had never been blessed with. This idea took—soon a perfect crowd surrounded him, when he commenced to inform them that he had for his own amusement, and for the benefit of the community at large, opened the good little game of 'sweat,' a little republican game that all could play at—"jist walk up, ride up, tumble up, any way to get up; then stake up and win a fortune—I don't belong to the aristocracy—I don't; I'm jist a plain old devil like all of you—I am! and if you jest bet on old Ned's little game, you'll win—you will! and if any one gets broke, I'll give him money to get a big drink, sure!" At this offer an *hombre* stuck down a quarter of a dollar and lost;—"There, Uncle Ned," says he, "I'm busted—just give us the four bits for the liquor!" Ned, to make his promise good, forked over the half-dollar, (the price of a drink), remarking, "you got me there a leetle—you did!" And thus continuing, he kept the crowd around him in a state of merriment that was new. To use one of Ned's phrases, "when them banks left, they were none of them broke—they wer'nt."

A Bear Encounter

Daniel Knower

Enterprising physician Daniel Knower of Albany, New York, set sail for California early in 1849 with twelve prefabricated houses to sell in San Francisco. After his arrival in August of that year, Knower sold the houses at a handsome profit, and later entered into the real estate speculation market.

Although he had no intent of mining himself, Knower did venture to the gold fields near Coloma to witness the lives of the miners there. He eventually published both his observations of the mine country and his experiences in the San Francisco area in his memoir *The Adventures of a Forty-Niner.* In the following excerpt, Knower relates the story of a miner who was attacked by a grizzly bear.

One warm afternoon my friend Mc and myself thought we would take a walk over to Pesedeo; that was about three miles to the Pacific Ocean. The seal rocks is where the sea lions or seals can always be seen. It was the entrance to the Golden Gates, where the roar of the Pacific Ocean is twice that of the Atlantic, it being six thousand miles broad, twice that of the Atlantic. On our way we stopped into a tent to get a drink of water. We found it occupied by three miners, one of whom was quite lame. I inquired of him what was the matter. He said his hip had been dislocated by the grizzlies. I asked him how it happened. He said they went up to the Trinity River to dig for gold. I knew that was the most remote gold river. He said they were lucky and found rich diggings, but after awhile their provisions gave out and

From Daniel Knower, *The Adventures of a Forty-Niner* (Albany, NY: Weed-Parsons, 1894).

they could not procure any unless they returned to the settlements. On their way, returning on horseback, they came to three grizzly bears grazing in a field. It was very dangerous to attack them, but they were very hungry. They thought if they could kill one of them it would supply them with meat, so they finally decided they would take their chances and fire on them, which they did, and wounded one. The other two took after the man whose hip was dislocated. He fled and came to a buckeye tree, the body of which slants, and he got up in it; the bears came on under it. After awhile they found they could not reach him. It being a low tree, one of them commenced climbing it after him. He thought his last hour had come; all the events of his life seemed to rush on his mind, and a picture of the old-fashioned spelling book, where the man plays dead on the bear, came before him, which I distinctly recollected. He thought his only chance was to drop from the tree and hold his breath, and play dead on the bear, which he did, and fell on his face. One bear grabbed him by the shoulders and the other by the ankle, and in pulling, dislocated his hip. He had a thick overcoat on which they tore to pieces. He held his breath. After awhile they went off and left him. After a little while he raised his head to see if they were gone, and they came trotting back and smelt him all over again, and went away again, he holding his breath. Then he laid a long time, fearing to move,[until] his companions came up [and roused him.] . . .

Bear Behavior

The State seal of California is Minerva, with a spear and shield and the grizzly bear at her feet. Before the discovery of gold they were quite numerous. They roamed in full possession, apparently, of the country—no one to molest them or make them afraid. It was a very formidable animal, weighing from seven to eight hundred pounds. When the rainy season set in, late in the fall, and the winter months, during which the grass commenced to grow, he fed on it in the valleys and fields, and became fat and powerful. In the spring, when the dry season set in and no rain for seven months, and fields dried up with a dusty brown, he fled to the tops of the mountains to browse on the leaves of the trees to support life until the next rainy season commenced. It is said he is not a ferocious animal if unmolested, and will not attack you if you let him alone, unless it is a she bear with cubs, or you shoot at them and wound them. They are very hard to kill. To be hit by a bullet has very little effect on them, unless hit in a vital spot. An acquaintance of mine was walking on a road in the interior and saw a big grizzly coming down the road in the opposite direction toward him. He knew it would not do to undertake to run. He had been posted on their natures, so he kept walking right on, as if he was undisturbed and had no fear, the bear coming nearer to him all the time, with his gait unchanged, or he his, until they passed each other, he looking the grizzly in the eye and treating each other with due respect and consideration as friends. As an illustration of their strength, an old Californian informed me that he knew of an instance where a grizzly came into a pack of live mules and took one off and carried it to his den and ate it. In corroboration of that fact, another man informed me that he saw a bear chasing a mule and fired on the bear and hit him, and the bear turned toward him, and the mule escaped.

Calamities in Sacramento

Dr. Jacob Stillman

Dr. Jacob Stillman arrived in San Francisco on August 5, 1849. Although he intended to accompany two shipboard acquaintances to the gold fields, he never made it. Instead, he settled in Sacramento, where he and Dr. John F. Morse established the city's first hospital in one of the few substantial buildings available.

Dr. Stillman's prior experience on the staff of Bellevue Hospital in New York City was undoubtedly insufficient to prepare him for the difficulties of frontier medicine. Writing home to his family, Dr. Stillman described all manner of death and destruction, much of which he was forced simply to endure rather than alleviate. The following excerpts from his collected letters offer but a few of the many calamities faced by this frontier physician.

December 23d.—We are at last in our new hospital building. It is, without doubt, the finest building in Sacramento. We have just opened, and are not yet complete in our arrangements. It is said to have cost the proprietors $15,000, and is no better than a barn at home that could be built for $2,000. It is finished inside with bleached muslin, except the main ward, which is a garret, with half windows on the side and two full windows at each gable.

From J.D.B. Stillman, letters of December 23, 1849–January 24, 1850, as reprinted in *The Gold Rush Letters of J.D.B. Stillman* (Palo Alto, CA: Lewis Osborne, 1967).

Sickness and Squalor

The people at home can have no conception of the amount of suffering in the vicinity of this city. Hundreds are encamped in tents, through the rains and storms, scantily supplied with food and covering. Many were driven from the mines for want of food, and are begging for employment, asking only subsistence. Yesterday there were twenty-five deaths. The sickness does not arise from the severity of the climate, which is no colder than November at home, but from a complication of causes. The intermittents of the Autumn are aggravated by overwork, scanty and bad food, disappointment, and home-sickness. Men, in the ravings of delirium, call upon friends who are far off, and, dying, mutter the names of their loved ones; men, wasting away with chronic disease, lose their manhood, and weep often, like children, to see their mothers once more. It is a great satisfaction to us to give them shelter and other things, for the want of which they are dying. Our enterprise commands the respect of the people, and we are determined to deserve it, so that if we are bankrupted it will be in a good cause. I fancy M—wishing to help us with her needle! Much need there was and is of needles, but we are becoming quite adept. I have sewed my fingers sore. There are a number of respectable women in the city, but we renegades from our own have no claim upon them, and are banded together like monks. There is nothing here to remind me of Christmas; the thermometer stands at "temperate," and rain is falling.

The Great Flood

January 11th, 1850.—We are witnesses of another act in the great drama of Californian adventures. Perhaps, before this reaches you, you will be informed of the calamitous flood that is now spreading destruction and death through the valley. We are all, about forty of us, in the upper story of our hospital—Dr. Morse and myself writing, Dr. Higgins (of Kentucky) reading Lamartine's "Raphael," the cook preparing something for breakfast, two or three other friends, quartered with us, talking in an under tone, some asleep, and a few patients muttering in delirium. A lone woman, sick and destitute, is curtained off in the corner of the room. She lost her husband on the plains, and has been supporting herself, with the assistance of a few friends, until the flood drove her out. She was brought here, with six men, the night before last. Some are dying on the floor; others, dead, are sewed up in blankets and sunk in the water in a room on the first floor. Dr. Morse pours some brandy in his ink, to give spirit to his letter; I pour from another bottle standing on the table, containing laudanum [tincture of opium], to quiet the apprehensions that mine may awaken; then we all laugh, and go on as before.

No Respite

January 12th.—The water is still rising. Tents, houses, boxes, barrels, horses, mules and cattle are sweeping by with the swollen torrent, that is now spread out in a vast sea farther than the eye can reach. There are few two-story houses, and as the water rose, which it did at the rate of six inches an hour, men were compelled to get outside. To-day there is no first floor in the city uncovered, and but for the vessels in the river, now all crowded with people, there is no telling what numbers must have perished.

What a night was that of the 9th of January! A warm rain from the south melted the snow on the Sierra, and the river during the day rose rapidly, and about midnight began to overflow its banks. We took warning and cleared our first floor as fast as we could. Fortunately, our second floor is spacious, and by midnight everything was off the lower floor that could be injured by water. As the flood continued to rise, we have continued to bring up things, so that as yet we have sustained no great loss, except in the white linings and curtains of our private wards, in which we have taken so much pride. Men continue to come, begging to be taken in, or bringing some valuables for safe keeping. Now that the doorways are inaccessible, they come in boats to the second-story windows. We take only the sick, and none such are refused. To-day we went out in a boat to find some blankets, but in vain. We returned with some drift-wood for fuel. All sorts of means are in use to get about—bakers' troughs, rafts, and India-rubber beds. There is no sound of gongs or dinner bells in the city. The yelling for help by some man on a roof, or clinging to some wreck—the howling of a dog abandoned by his master—the boisterous revelry of men in boats, who find all they want to drink floating free about them—make the scene one never to be forgotten. After dark we see only one or two lights in the second city of California. I think the worst is now over, though the water is still gaining on us. The wind may rise and cause a heavy sea; this I conceive to be our greatest danger. We are in an ocean of water, and our building may be too frail to resist a strong wind with waves. The steamer *Senator* carried down all the people that could crowd on board, and we are in hopes of aid from below in time. I have some misgivings about our fate, but sure I am that we will not desert the sick, and if we are swept away, we will all go together.

It is late, and for two days and nights I have not slept. I shall now lie down, and if the worst comes, I have taken precautions to have you get this letter.

Burying the Dead

Sunday, January 13th.—The water has not risen or fallen since yesterday, nor have we had any high wind. Yesterday we found it necessary to bury the dead. I spoke a whale boat that was passing, made all agreement for the use of it in the afternoon for $40, and deposited three bodies in it. They had been sewed up in blankets and sunk in the first story. We fished them up with a hook and line, and laid them in the bottom of the boat—two white men and a negro. Mr. Mulford— a Yale College man, who is staying with us and watching the sick, and in other ways paying his board—Mr. Cannon, the druggist, and myself, with the two sailors owning the boat, started for land, which we could see with a glass from our window in a south-easterly direction from the town. Of course, coffins were out of the question, and we dug a large, square grave, at the foot of an oak. The two white men we placed side by side, and the black man across at their feet. In digging the grave we found a large root of the tree intersecting the pit in both directions, as if two sticks had been placed across each other at right angles, and had grown together in that position. By chopping it off at the ends, the root formed a perfect cross, which we planted at the head of the grave, and then covered the mound with the soft, green sod. The day was beautiful; the meadow larks and blackbirds were flying about us in great numbers, and along the shores wild geese were feeding on the young grass. Sutter's Fort was about a mile distant.

To-day two more poor emaciated remains have been deposited below. The weather is cooler and the water is falling a little. The vessels on the river are all crowded with people, and some cases of typhus or ship-fever have occurred. The high ground near the fort is covered with tents, dogs and cattle. In this vicinity there has been but little loss of human life by drowning, that I have heard of, though it seemed unavoidable. Had there been many women and children, results would have been otherwise. Cattle, however, have perished in immense numbers.

Unable to Cope

On my return to-day from a visit to the bark *Phoenix* to see a typhoid-fever patient, I found one of those admitted yesterday furiously insane. He broke a window and tried to jump out into the water, and, hailing a boat, offered fifty dollars to be taken to the bark *Mousam,* from which vessel he had been sent. Dr. Morse was making arrangements for putting him in a straight-jacket, and I went to him to find some solution for so sudden a paroxysm. He had seen the dying around him, and the dead carried out in their burial blankets—for everything has to be done in one room—had become melancholy, and finally maniacal. I talked sympathizingly with him and tried to win his confidence. As I leaned over him he looked steadfastly in my face for a long time, and then said, "Doctor, you have an honest face, but, O, my God!"—and he covered his face with his hands for some time; then, in a tone of awful mystery, he said there were strange things going on in the house. He spoke of his wife and children in Hudson, in a frenzy of affection, and said he should die and never see them more. When I turned from his bed, he took my hand in both of his, and begged me to be his friend, as I had a wife that I loved. I assured him that I would do anything in the world for him, if he would keep quiet and not disturb the other sick people. "O! Doctor, you can do all I want done for me. You see, I could jump from that window and drown myself, but then my family would lose the benefit of a life insurance for $1,000." "Now," said he in a whisper that could not be heard at the next bed, "you can arrange it for me so that there will be no trouble. You can give me something in a cup of tea that will let me go, and my family will be all right." I assured him, in the same confidential tone, that the thing could be easily done if he was fully convinced that it was best; but the danger to me would be from his repentance when it would be too late, and in the agonies of death he would betray me; that I was not in a hurry to die, and, least of all, by the halter. He said he would keep the secret, and called on God to witness. After allowing him to persuade me for some time, I consented to grant his request on certain conditions. He should, when the tea was prepared, drink it without speaking, lie down immediately and make no sound, though he should suffer the tortures of the damned. The conditions were accepted. I then prepared a cup of black tea, and in it dissolved a full dose of the sulphate of morphia [morphine], and with an air of unconcern I handed him the tea. He took it in his hand as he rose to a sitting posture in his bed, and, looking with close scrutiny into my face, he said: "You are fooling me!" "Give me the cup," I said, with an air of offended honor that gave him to understand that he had violated his oath. He instantly drank the contents of the cup, and fell back upon his pillow with his eyes closed. When I returned to him a half hour after, he was in a deep sleep. It is now two o'clock in the morning, my watch is up, my maniac is sleeping heavily, and I must sleep too.

A Near Drowning

January 14th.—My portfolio arrived this afternoon by the last trip of the India-rubber bed, by means of which we have established a system of internal navigation between the various apartments on the first floor. We came near losing our apothecary to-day. He was experimenting with a new mode of navigation in the main hall of the building. He had procured a butter barrel, which had a square hole cut in the side big enough to admit his body by a little squeezing, and started off from the stairs, holding on to the siding for support. He had not gone many feet when he capsized and hung head down, unable to extricate himself. Peter, who is a good swimmer, went to his rescue, and Cannon came out looking as if he was ashamed that he was not drowned.

The water is falling a little. I have been reading to my maniac some passages of your last letter. He is quite rational and calm to-day, but it does not answer to lead his thoughts toward his home.

January 23d.—The water has left the floor, though it is three or four feet in depth around the house. We found four barrels of pork, one of beef, and a case of wine on our premises, that were not there when the flood came. We don't hesitate to appropriate them as a contribution to the support of the many destitute people thrown upon us.

January 24th.—All things go on swimmingly, but not in the same sense that they did early in the month. To-day, six more poor emaciated victims of chronic diarrhoea were brought to us. They were found accidentally in a canvas house, when the inundation had reached their beds, and for two weeks have been lying on the wet ground, without fire: two days, they tell us, they were without food. We have purchased a bale of blankets, and are able to throw away many old ones, as we cannot get them washed. We have demanded assistance from the City Council, for as yet we have not had a dollar from any quarter since the flood. Thus far we have had to pay our expenses by a few pay-patients and outside practice. Of those who are destitute, and who get well, we take their notes; if they die, we take a check on Heaven.

Frontier Justice

J.D. Borthwick

Artist J.D. Borthwick, a native of Edinburgh, Scotland, was living in New York City in May of 1851 when he found himself suddenly "seized with the California fever." Although the most sensational accounts of the gold discoveries in the west had already begun to subside, he immediately embarked on a small ship and made his journey to California by way of Panama.

Borthwick would spend three years prospecting at various digging grounds in the California mining country. Upon his return to Scotland in 1857, he published a memoir of his adventures, *Three Years in California*. Borthwick illustrated the book with eight of his own lithographs, and he focused much of his attention on the customs and social life of the mining locale. In the following selection, Borthwick describes the administration of Lynch Law, the prevailing form of justice on the frontier.

A few weeks before my arrival there, Downieville had been the scene of great excitement on one of those occasions when the people took on themselves the administration and execution of justice.

A Mexican woman one forenoon had, without provocation, stabbed a miner to the heart, killing him on the spot. The news of the murder spread rapidly up and down the river, and a vast concourse of miners immediately began to collect in the town.

The woman, an hour or two after she committed the mur-

From J.D. Borthwick, *Three Years in California, 1851–1854* (Edinburgh: Blackwood & Sons, 1857).

der, was formally tried by a jury of twelve, found guilty, and condemned to be hung that afternoon. The case was so clear that it admitted of no doubt, several men having been witnesses of the whole occurrence; and the woman was hung accordingly, on the bridge in front of the town, in presence of many thousand people.

Lynch Law a Necessity in California

For those whose ideas of the proper mode of administering criminal law are only acquired from an acquaintance with the statistics of crime and its punishment in such countries as England, where a single murder excites horror throughout the kingdom, and is for days a matter of public interest, where judicial corruption is unknown, where the instruments of the law are ubiquitous, and its action all but infallible— for such persons it may be difficult to realise a state of things which should render it necessary, or even excusable, that any number of irresponsible individuals should exercise a power of life and death over their fellow-men.

And no doubt many sound theories may be brought forward against the propriety of administering Lynch Law; but California, in the state of society which then existed, and in view of the total inefficiency, or worse than inefficiency, of the established courts of justice, was no place for theorising upon abstract principles. Society had to protect itself by the most practical and unsophisticated system of retributive justice, quick in its action, and whose operation, being totally divested of all mystery and unnecessary ceremony, was perfectly comprehensible to the meanest understanding—a system inconsistent with public safety in old countries— unnecessary, in fact, where the machinery of the law is perfect in all its parts—but at the same time one which men most naturally adopt in the absence of all other protection; and any one who lived in the mines of California at that time is bound gratefully to acknowledge that the feeling of security of life and person which he there enjoyed was due in a great measure to his knowledge of the fact that this admirable institution of Lynch Law was in full and active operation.

There were in California the elite of the most desperate and consummate scoundrels from every part of the world; and the unsettled state of the country, the wandering habits of the mining population, scattered, as they were, all over the mountains, and frequently carrying an amount of gold on their persons inconvenient from its very weight, together with the isolated condition of many individuals, strangers to every one around them, and who, if put out of the way, would never have been missed—all these things tended apparently to render the country one where such ruffians would have ample room to practise their villany. But, thanks to Lynch Law, murders and robberies, numerous as they were, were by no means of such frequent occurrence as might have been expected, considering the opportunities and temptations afforded to such a large proportion of the population, who were only restrained from violence by a wholesome regard for the safety of their own necks.

An Effective Deterrent

And after all, the fear of punishment of death is the most effectual preventive of crime. To the class of men among whom murderers are found, it is probably the only feeling which deters them, and its influence is unconsciously felt even by those whose sense of right and wrong is not yet so dead as to allow them to contemplate the possibility of their committing a murder. In old States, however, fear of the punishment of death does not act with its full force on the mind of the intending criminal, for the idea of the expiation of his crime on the scaffold has to be preceded in his imagination by all the mysterious and tedious formalities of the law, in the uncertainty of which he is apt to flatter himself that he will by some means get an acquittal; and even if convicted, the length of time which must elapse before his ultimate punishment, together with the parade and circumstance with which it is attended, divests it in a great measure of the feelings of horror which it is intended to arouse.

But when Lynch Law prevails, it strikes terror to the heart of the evil-doer. He has no hazy and undefined view of his ultimate fate in the distant future, but a vivid picture is before him of the sure and speedy consequence of crime. The formalities and delays of the law, which are instituted for the protection of the people, are for the same reason abolished, and the criminal knows that, instead of being tried by the elaborate and intricate process of law, his very ignorance of which leads him to over-estimate his chance of escape, he will have to stand before a tribunal of men, who will try him, not by law, but by hard, straightforward common-sense, and from whom he can hope for no other verdict than that which his own conscience awards him; while execution follows so close upon sentence, that it forms, as it were, but part of the same ceremony: for Californians were eminently practical and earnest; what they meant to do they did "right

Hanged and Whipped

Indiana native Jacob Harlan arrived in California with his family in 1846, well ahead of the gold rush. He worked at various jobs and locations, including milk and livery businesses in San Francisco, storekeeping in the gold camps near Coloma and Sonora, and farming and ranching in and around San Jose. While in San Jose in early 1849, young Jacob and his cousin George found themselves face to face with the savageness of frontier justice.

On March 6, 1849, my cousin, George, and myself being in San Jose, we saw three men hanged, and three others whipped. The cause of their execution was their having robbed and tried to murder a German, who was returning from the mines. He had three thousand five hundred dollars, and some way the robbers knew it. He had camped at a slough three miles west from Slocumb's ferry, which was the lowest ferry on the San Joaquin river. Shortly after he had camped, three men also camped about a mile from him, and before sundown these were joined by three more men. These men had followed the German to rob him. Three of them went to do the job, and the other three stayed in camp.

off," with all their might, and as if they really meant to do it; and Lynch Law was administered with characteristic promptness and decision. Sufficient time, however, or at least what was considered to be sufficient time, was always granted to the criminal to prepare for death. Very frequently he was not hanged till the day after his trial.

Efficient and Expedient Punishment

An execution, of course, attracted an immense crowd, but it was conducted with as little parade as possible. Men were hung in the readiest way which suggested itself—on a bough of the nearest tree, or on a tree close to the spot where the murder was committed. In some instances the criminal was run up by a number of men, all equally sharing the

---

The plan was to rob him, but not kill him. After they got his money and his gun, one of them named Fred said, "a dead man tells no tales," and shot him. He fell as if dead, but when the thieves were gone he got up, and wounded as he was, walked fifteen miles to Livermore's rancho. Livermore took care of him, and sent to San Jose and notified alcalde Dimmick, who took steps to capture the robbers. Livermore's son, who bore his father's message to the alcalde, got to San Jose in advance, and they carelessly rode into the town, and were taken. They were tried by the alcalde and a jury, and found guilty of robbery and attempt to murder, and the three who did the robbing and shooting were sentenced to be hanged, and the other three, as accomplices, were sentenced to receive one hundred and thirty lashes. We saw the three hanged, but did not see the whipping. We saw the men after they had been whipped, and from their condition I concluded that if it had been my case I would have preferred to be hanged. Being hanged is a miserable way to get out of this life, and I resolved never again to see more of it, or of whipping either.

Jacob Harlan, *California '46 to '88.* San Francisco: Bancroft, 1888.

hangman's duty; on other occasions, one man was appointed to the office of executioner, and a drop was extemporised by placing the culprit on his feet on the top of an empty box or barrel, under the bough of a tree, and at the given signal the box was knocked away from under him.

Not an uncommon mode was, to mount the criminal on a horse or mule, when, after the rope was adjusted, a cut of a whip was administered to the back of the animal, and the man was left suspended.

Petty thefts, which were of very rare occurrence, were punished by so many lashes with a cow-hide, and the culprit was then banished [from] the camp. A man who would commit a petty theft was generally such a poor miserable devil as to excite compassion more than any other feeling, and not unfrequently, after his chastisement, a small subscription was raised for him, to help him along till he reached some other diggings.

Theft or robbery of any considerable amount, however, was a capital crime; and horse-stealing, to which the Mexicans more particularly devoted themselves, was invariably a hanging matter.

Lynch Law had hitherto prevailed only in the mines; but about this time it had been found necessary to introduce it also in San Francisco. The number of murders and robberies committed there had of late increased to an alarming extent; and from the laxity and corruption of those entrusted with the punishment and prevention of crime, the criminal part of the population carried on their operations with such a degree of audacity, and so much apparent confidence in the impunity which they enjoyed, that society, in the total inefficiency of the system which it had instituted for its defence and preservation, threatened to become a helpless prey to the well-organised gang of ruffians who were every day becoming more insolent in their career.

Vigilance Committee Formed

At last human nature could stand it no longer, and the people saw the necessity of acting together in self-defence.

A Committee of Vigilance was accordingly formed, composed chiefly of the most prominent and influential citizens, and which had the cordial approval, and the active support, of nearly the entire population of the city.

The first action of the Committee was to take two men out of gaol who had already been convicted of murder and robbery, but for the execution of whose sentence the experience of the past afforded no guarantee. These two men, when taken out of the gaol, were driven in a coach and four at full gallop through the town, and in half an hour they were swinging from the beams projecting over the windows of the store which was used as the committee-rooms.

The Committee, during their reign, hanged four or five men, all of whom, by their own confessions, deserved hanging half-a-dozen times over. Their confessions disclosed a most extensive and wealthy organisation of villany, in which several men of comparatively respectable position were implicated. These were the projectors and designers of elaborate schemes of wholesale robbery, which the more practical members of the profession executed under their superintendence; and in the possession of some of these men there were found exact plans of the stores of many of the wealthiest merchants, along with programmes of robberies to come off.

The operations of the Committee were not confined to hanging alone; their object was to purge the city of the whole herd of malefactors which infested it. Most of them, however, were panic-struck at the first alarm of Lynch Law, and fled to the mines; but many of those who were denounced in the confessions of their brethren were seized by the Committee, and shipped out of the country. Several of the most distinguished scoundrels were graduates from our penal colonies; and to put a stop, if possible, to the further immigration of such characters, the Committee boarded every ship from New South Wales as she arrived, and satisfied themselves of the respectability of each passenger before allowing him to land.

The authorities, of course, were greatly incensed at the action of the Vigilance Committee in taking from them the power they had so badly used, but they could do nothing against the unanimous voice of the people, and had to submit with the best grace they could.

The Committee, after a very short but very active reign, had so far accomplished their object of suppressing crime, and driving the scum of the population out of the city, that they resigned their functions in favour of the constituted authorities; at the same time, however, intimating that they remained alert, and only inactive so long as the ordinary course of law was found effectual.

A Rough Spectacle

William Perkins

> Born in Toronto, Canada, in 1827, William Perkins was living
> in Cincinnati when he departed for the gold country in 1849.
> After his arrival in San Francisco on June 9, he made his way
> to the southern mines at a time when most of the prospectors
> were headed northward. By chance he soon settled in Sonora,
> where he became immediately less interested in making a for-
> tune and more interested in the colorful society that sur-
> rounded him.
>
> Perhaps Perkins's Canadian heritage attracted him to the
> city; Sonora had become somewhat of a Mecca for foreign-
> born immigrants. The city was consequently more varied in
> its culture than its counterparts to the north, and it therefore
> made a highly interesting subject for Perkins's perceptive
> eyes and ears. In the following selection from his memoir,
> Perkins describes the particularly unusual amusement of
> bull and bear baiting that occupied the curiosities of
> Sonora's "half-civilized" citizens.

Sunday, Twenty Third. We have lately had introduced in
town a novel amusement for the million; something too,
quite in keeping with the wild or half-civilized state we are
in, and the rough semi-savage propensities of our population. I allude to Bull and Bear baiting.

In Mexico I have seen Bull fighting in all its barbarous
perfection. I have seen eight wild bulls slain in one afternoon, in the arena, and beautiful maidens greeting with a
never-tired enthusiasm, the skill of the graceful *Matador,*

From the memoirs of William Perkins as reprinted in *Three Years in California*, by William
Perkins (Berkeley: University of California Press, 1924).

as he gives the poor tired brute the *coup de grace.* It is difficult to say which of the two descriptions of combats is the most cruel. For my part, the contest between man and beast excites in me more sympathy from the fact that the latter fights at a disadvantage, and is always the victim; while between animals the combat is at all events, more or less on terms of equality, and when one of the combatants is conquered, at least he dies gloriously on the field of battle after a brave struggle, and is not killed traitorously and cowardly after having been baited and tortured by a host of tormentors for the gratification of a cruel and eager crowd. Yes, of the two I prefer witnessing a combat between beasts, unless more equal terms are given to the poor brutes in their contests with man, so as to give them a chance of coming off victoriously.

Formidable Foes

The great Bear of the Rocky Mountains, better known as the "Grizzly," makes a very formidable antagonist for a good sized untamed bull. At liberty, they shun, but do not fear each other, like the Royal Tiger and the Lion in the East; each conscious of his own strength, yet each tacitly acknowledging a certain respect for that of his adversary, they agree to a system of non-intervention.

The bears are taken in pitfalls, and, placed in iron cages, are sold to the owners of Bull rings, sometimes at as high a figure as two thousand dollars. There is quite a demand for them in San Francisco and the towns lower down on the coast.

Each Sunday there is a combat between Bears and Bulls in the arena of Sonora, and, as the former are chained, they often get the worst of the fight, although the latter are generally so badly bitten that they are killed immediately afterwards.

I will now describe the scene in the Arena today which I witnessed, and the fatal circumstances which attended it will probably have the effect of obliging the Authorities to put an end to similar performances for the future.

The owners of the Bull Ring had secured a magnificent

Bear at a cost of one thousand dollars. He was as large as a good-sized bullock, and weighed probably thirteen or fourteen hundred pounds. The inside of the huge tent was crowded; upwards of two thousand persons were present.

Bruin was secured with a free length of about ten feet of chain, and stalked to and fro with a savage dignity, stopping every now and then to look round upon and utter a low growl at the assembled multitude. Three bulls were turned into the ring, but were evidently scared and fought shy. The bear was turned over two or three times, but received no injury, and one of the bulls got pretty badly treated; all three were worsted and frightened. They were withdrawn amid the hisses of the spectators.

The Battle Begins

A splendid animal was now let in. This was a huge black bull, a magnificent fellow. His whole frame appeared to be quivering with rage; his tail was extended straight out in a line with the vertebrae, and his eyes, one could almost fancy, were flashing fire. He sprung with a single bound into the middle of the ring, and looked round proudly and fearlessly on the crowd; then commenced a low bellowing, and tossing the dirt up with his hoofs. In a few seconds he had caught sight of his antagonist, and immediately without the slightest hesitation, made a rush at him. Master Bruin curled himself up into a ball, and the furious bull rushed over him, missing his stroke. The bear, with wonderful quickness, sprung up at this moment, and caught the bull by the thigh with his teeth, and inflicted a ghastly wound. The noble animal gave a roar of mingled agony and rage, turned round, and, catching his adversary with his tremendous horns, raised him, notwithstanding his enormous weight, and made him perform a somerset that was only bounded by the length of the chain. The bear fell with a shock that seemed sufficient to break every bone in his body; but no; quick as a flash he had again given the bull a severe wound in the haunch, and the latter moved off to a little distance to breathe. In a few moments, he again made a gallant attack, again gave the bear a tremendous goring, and was again driven off by the frightful wounds he received from the teeth of the Grizzly, who appeared to keep his temper better than his antagonist, and consequently fought under greater advantage.

Four times did the brave brute make a desperate attack, and, although the bear was badly hurt, the bull always got the worst of it, until cowed and scared by a last fearful bite, when the bear caught him by the head, he turned, and collecting all his remaining strength, with one bound he topped the palisades and dropped like something more than a hot potato amongst a crowd of Mexicans. The terror was intense; such a scampering! such an outcry! Several people were badly hurt and one was gored to death by the infuriated animal, who however, more anxious to escape himself than to show more fight, quickly cleared the crowd and fled up the mountains, pursued by a score of horsemen with their *lassos*.

More Brutality

While this was going on outside, another interesting scene was being exhibited within the tent. The bear was lying panting and apparently exhausted, with his huge blood-red tongue hanging half a yard out of his mouth. A Mexican approached him with a bucket of water to pour on him, and thinking the animal was extended at the full length of his chain, walked close up to him. But Master Bruin was only "playing 'possum." With a sudden spring he caught the unfortunate fellow in his arms, threw him down, and with one effort of his tremendous jaws crushed the man's thigh as if it were a willow stick. We distinctly heard the snapping of the brute's teeth as they closed through the flesh and bone. In another minute, ay, in a quarter of a minute, all would have been over.

Then followed a scene that could only have taken place in California, and that, in truth, requires the testimony of an eye witness to be believed. The man was under the bear, and the beast was *crunching* his leg with his teeth. In an instant a score of revolvers were drawn and *fired*. The bear was riddled with balls, and the man was untouched! The most fatal shot was in the bear's head, and this proceeded from a man standing above the crowd on the topmost bench, and he fired over the heads of two or three hundred people. At least, this person claims the honor of having sent a ball within a few inches of the Mexican's body into the bear's head. The leg of the wounded man had to be amputated immediately, but it is doubtful if he lived.

It is well that the Authorities intend putting a stop to these brutal exhibitions. They do no good, but keep the town in an uproar every Sunday, induce drinking and gambling, and, as was evidenced today, endanger life. It seems a miracle that so few people were hurt by the catastrophe of the bull jumping into a dense mass of people; but the poor animal, being as much frightened as were the bipeds, took advantage of the openings offered him by the flying crowd, and sought more eagerly to escape than to revenge his wrongs.

This will, I suppose, be the last exhibition of the kind we shall have here. In San Francisco, San José and Monterey, they are still allowed, but in these places they are not productive of so much scandal and vice as in the mines.

The San Francisco Fire of 1851

L.J. Hall

Responding to the gold fever that was spreading along the East
Coast in late 1848, a band of adventure-seeking citizens of
Hartford, Connecticut formed the Hartford Union Mining and
Trading Company. The joint venture actually purchased and
outfitted its own ship, the *Henry Lee*, for the journey to California. The idea was to bring supplies to the mining country for
trading purposes and to prospect for gold along the way.

Company member L.J. Hall, who was a printer by trade,
documented his and his associates' forays into the gold fields
after the party arrived in September of 1849. Hall eventually
settled in San Francisco, where he found full-time work as a
printer for the *Courier*. In the following excerpt from his self-
published book *Around the Horn in '49: Journal of the Hartford Union Mining and Trading Company*, Hall recounts the
fateful evening of May 1, 1851.

Since I have been occupied in the San Francisco Courier
office, at a salary of $55 a week, for the last six or eight
weeks my work has been confined to the day instead of the
night. This was every way more desirable. It gave me the
evenings for study and pleasure, and the nights for sleep. I
attended a night school taught by a Spaniard, in which the
Spanish language was the sole study. William Rand,[1] the

1. William Rand returned to the East and made a fortune in Chicago, under the firm name
of "Rand, McNally Co."

From L.J. Hall, *Around the Horn in '49: Journal of the Hartford Union Mining and Trading Company* (Wethersfield, CT: L.J. Hall, 1898).

foreman of the jobbing department, was my fellow-student. Our wages were paid in gold coin every Monday. We found out the truth of the old adage, "A bird in hand is worth two in the bush." The jingling of the coin in the pocket was musical in the day, but in the evening it sounded "*doloroso*," [dull] lest some highwayman would be attracted by its music. During the few months past I had not met with any of the Henry Lee Company until the third day of this month, when, if my memory serves me correctly, Giles P. Kellogg, of Rockville, Conn., gave me a call. He had just returned from the Marquesas Island with a cargo of fruit, which had found a quick and profitable market. He shared my room, sleeping, from choice, in his blankets on the floor. Having deposited his gold in some bank, or place of security, we started out to view the scenes of the city.

The Alarm Sounds

We walked through the principal streets, and about 8 o'clock we were quietly viewing the attractions surrounding the plaza. Suddenly the alarm of fire was given on all sides of the square. The strong winds forced the fire and smoke in a rapid current down the wooden culverts of Sacramento street as swift as a race horse. The want of water, and of an organized fire department, soon placed the fire beyond control. Excited men were running in all directions. The current of the fire was toward our lodging room. We both rushed forward to save, if possible, our effects. By the time we came in sight of the building we found the front and roof already blazing, and the door-frame charring with the heat. The live coals were falling around us. Pulling up our coat collars, and down our hats, we broke through the door, and hastily gathering our blankets, leaving all our gathered gems and valuables to the mercy of the devouring elements, we retraced our steps to the street. There we separated, Mr. Kellogg to look after the safety of his deposit, and I to the Courier office, to see what could be done for its protection. My course was turned several times by being cut off by the devastation of the fire.

The office of the San Francisco Courier was in the upper

room of a large three story brick building. The walls, two feet in thickness at the bottom, gradually tapered to one foot at the top. The windows had thick iron shutters, and the lower doors were also of iron. It was built for a fire-proof building. Upon reaching the office I found only one young compositor, by the name of Saunders. The forms from which the evening edition were printed still lay on the composing stone. I immediately locked them securely, with the idea that they would be lowered from a window to the ground and be found ready for the next day's edition. The proprietor came in and said my labor was unnecessary, as the building was fire-proof, and if I had anything of value it would be safer there than any other part of the city. I had seen the ravages of the fire upon my way to the office, and expressed great doubt of its withstanding the concentrated current of fire. As I descended the stairs, a man confined to his bed with sickness asked my opinion of the safety of the building, which I frankly gave; and through his persistent urging, he was removed from it. The janitor, confident in the safety of the fire-proof block, was seen just before the building fell, on the top, but was devoured by the fire, so that no vestige of his remains could be discovered. No words of mine can describe the quick, destructive power of that current of fire, which was concentrated by the increased velocity of the wind into a burning arrow against wood, brick and stone. A large corrugated iron building, into which were crowded a number of men for safety, two or three squares distant, the moment this arrow of fire reached it, so rolled or bent that the iron doors and window shutters could not be unlocked, and escape from it was impossible, and the men perished.

Seeking Refuge

Telegraph Hill was sought by multitudes as the only place of safety on land, and the waters of the bay by those who had boats. The former was suggested as our only retreat. Mr. Saunders and myself, with our blankets, endeavored to reach it. Twice our way was cut off by the work of the devouring elements.

On our way we passed crowds of men crazed by the liquors they had obtained by pillaging from the saloons or restaurants—while other crowds were ransacking the dry goods stores and clothing houses for suits, cloths and blankets, and the hardware stores for pistols and other weapons. The firing of pistols, the throwing of champagne bottles, the carousal of the intoxicated, the screams of women, and the orgies of the uncontrollable multitude, were frightful scenes that will never be forgotten by those who witnessed them.

We found a place somewhat distant from the strollers, and throwing down our blankets, we rested on them and looked over the burning city. This event turned my thoughts to the whole series of experiences through which I had passed in California, and even in the life preceding. I was deeply impressed that it was a Providence—a voice that called me to a different vocation of life. Upon entering the mines, one evening I had withdrawn from my companions for reflection and prayer. The prayer voiced one petition that was followed by a vision of the lives of two characters. That petition was, that God in his providences would meet me with obstructions to the plans I made until I had found the right place for my life's work. The flood, the fire in the mountains, the failure of mining schemes, the losses of honestly-earned wages, the fraud of the auctioneer, and this last disappointment of plans I had made—all were an answer to that prayer. The resolution to immediately leave California and pursue a course of study that would prepare me for my life's labors, was communicated to my companion. As soon as the wharves were in condition for us to visit the vessels that lay beside them, we engaged passage on the bark Florida. On the 6th of May, 1891, we left San Francisco for our homes in the East.

Chronology

1839

August: Immigrant John Sutter arrives in the California Territory and settles inland at the convergence of the Sacramento and American Rivers. He obtains a fifty-thousand-acre land grant from Mexican governor Alvarado and begins building his empire, which he christens New Helvetia, but which is more commonly known as Sutter's Fort. The settlement becomes a major trading hub for the region.

1841

November 4: John Bidwell leads the first group of California pioneers into the San Joaquin Valley after a six-month overland journey from Independence, Missouri.

1842

March: Rancher Francisco Lopez finds gold in the San Fernando Hills thirty miles northwest of Los Angeles while digging wild onions. Although prospectors from the immediate area converge on the site, there is not enough gold, or water to extract it, to fuel a major gold rush. By 1845, the site is largely exhausted.

1845

July: James Marshall arrives at Sutter's Fort on a wagon train from Oregon. Having had construction experience, he begins to complete building projects for Sutter's Fort.

1846

May 13: War breaks out between Mexico and the United States.

July 7: The U.S. Pacific Fleet lands at Monterey, where Commodore John Sloat raises the American flag and claims California for the United States.

1847

January 13: The war over California ends when the Cahuenga Capitulation is signed by U.S. captain John Fremont and Mexican general Pico.

May 16: Sutter dispatches Marshall into the foothills to locate a site for a sawmill. Marshall finds a good spot in a wooded valley on the South Fork of the American River known to the Native Americans as Culluma.

August 27: Sutter and Marshall enter into a written agreement to build the mill at the site in the Culluma (Coloma) Valley. Sutter would provide the money and labor, and Marshall would provide the expertise.

September: Marshall begins work on the sawmill in the Coloma Valley.

1848

January 24: Marshall discovers what he believes to be gold while testing the newly completed millrace. Crude preliminary tests confirm his suspicions, and he sets off to inform Sutter.

January 28: Marshall arrives at Sutter's Fort, and after completing more reliable tests, he confirms that his discovery is gold.

February 2: The war with Mexico officially ends with the signing of the Treaty of Guadalupe Hidalgo. California becomes an official U.S. territory.

March: Although Sutter and Marshall have attempted to keep the discovery a secret, word spreads quickly in the region. A separate mining camp springs up outside Coloma, and Marshall begins to lose his laborers to the gold fields.

March 11: Marshall completes the sawmill, which will operate for five years before being scrapped for lumber to build cabins.

March 15: The first story of the discovery is printed in a San Francisco newspaper, but most people meet the report with skepticism.

April: John Bidwell strikes it rich at Bidwell's Bar. A messenger leaves San Francisco for the East Coast with news of the gold discovery.

May: Eight hundred prospectors have gathered in the valleys and gulches surrounding Sutter's Mill in Coloma; some have already located rich strikes. Gold is also discovered on the Yuba River, and boomtowns begin to spring up in the region. The people of San Francisco, finally convinced that the reports are true, begin a mass exodus for the diggings.

June: With two thousand miners now working the foothills, San Francisco becomes almost deserted. The first official reports of the discovery are dispatched to U.S. government representatives on the East Coast.

July: There are an estimated four thousand prospectors now in the mines. California military governor R.B. Mason tours the Coloma diggings and confirms the discovery. Prospectors from Southern California begin to head north.

August: Unconfirmed reports of the discovery reach the East Coast. Mining camps begin to spring up in other areas, such as Carson Creek and Sonora.

September: Washington, D.C., receives official confirmation of the discovery.

October: Word of the discovery reaches Mexico.

November: Ships loaded with gold seekers begin departing from East Coast ports.

December 5: In a speech to Congress, President Polk confirms the discovery of gold in California. Meanwhile, John Sutter and James Marshall, having been overrun by miners, sell their interests in the Coloma Valley.

December 23: An Australian newspaper prints a story on the gold discovery, and hundreds of prospectors subsequently set sail for California.

1849

January: Europeans begin to ship off for the mines in California.

February 28: The first forty-niners land in San Francisco aboard the steamship *California.*

Spring: As winter eases, new mining camps spring up.

May: Wagon trains set out from St. Joseph and Independence, Missouri, for the overland trip to California. Prospectors from Sonora, Mexico, begin heading north to the mines.

July: The first wagon train arrives in the Sacramento Valley. By this time, six hundred vessels filled with gold seekers have landed in San Francisco.

October: The first European immigrants arrive in California. Boomtowns continue to spring up throughout the gold region.

November: Although not yet a state in the Union, California ratifies a constitution, elects a governor, and names lawmakers.

Winter: Over eighty thousand gold seekers arrive from all over the world during the year. The cities of San Francisco and Sacramento are forced to grow rapidly to accommodate the hoards, who cannot survive the winter in the wilderness. The population of San Francisco alone reaches an estimated one hundred thousand residents by the year's end.

1850

March: Mexican miners discover gold north of Sonora.

April: The territorial government initiates a monthly $20.00 Foreign Miners Tax, mainly to discriminate against Mexican and Chinese miners.

Summer: The gold region continues to expand, with discoveries at Kanaka Creek, Grass Valley, Onion Valley, and Indian Camp.

September 9: California officially becomes the thirty-first state of the Union.

Winter: Over ninety thousand immigrants arrive during the year.

1851

February: Hard-rock mining begins after gold-bearing quartz is found at Amador Creek.

March 14: The Foreign Miners Tax is temporarily repealed.

April: Most of the mining claims are taken, and new deposits of gold become extremely difficult to find. When gold is discovered in Australia and Oregon, many miners leave for what seem like greener pastures.

1852

May 4: A license fee of $3.00 is assessed to all foreign miners.

End of Year: John Sutter has lost his entire empire. He leaves California a bankrupt and dejected man.

1853

March: Hydraulic mining is initiated in California when E.E. Matteson first forces water though a nozzle to wash away a gravel bank.

1854

Autumn: Gold is discovered on the Kern River in Southern California, leading some miners to abandon the already depleted northern mines.

1855

The rich surface deposits of gold have been largely exhausted. River mining begins to account for much of the state's output of gold.

1859

July 1: The *Nevada Journal* publishes reports of the discovery of gold and silver at the Comstock Lode in Nevada. During the same year, gold is also discovered in Boulder Canyon, Colorado. For many historians, the resulting exodus of miners from California to these newer finds marks the end of the gold rush.

For Further Research

Books

Faxon Dean Atherton, *The California Diary of Faxon Dean Atherton, 1836–1839.* San Francisco: California Historical Society, 1964.

Edwin Beilharz, *We Were 49ers! Chilean Accounts of the California Gold Rush.* Pasadena, CA: Ward Ritchie Press, 1976.

John Bidwell, *In California Before the Gold Rush.* Los Angeles: Ward Ritchie Press, 1948.

Peter J. Blodgett, *Land of Golden Dreams: California in the Gold Rush Decade, 1848–1858.* San Marino, CA: Huntington Library, 1999.

John W. Caughey, ed., *Rushing for Gold.* Berkeley: University of California Press, 1949.

Charles W. Churchill, *Fortunes Are for the Few: Letters of a Forty-Niner.* San Diego: San Diego Historical Society, 1977.

Dwight L. Clarke, *William Tecumseh Sherman: Gold Rush Banker.* San Francisco: California Historical Society, 1969.

Julian Dana, *Sutter of California: A Biography.* New York: Halcyon House, 1938.

James Delavan, *Notes on California and the Placers.* Oakland, CA: Biobooks, 1956.

Richard Dillon, *Exploring the Mother Lode Country.* Pasadena, CA: Ward Ritchie Press, 1974.

Thomas J. Farnham, *Travels in California.* Oakland, CA: Biobooks, 1947.

Joseph Haer, ed., *Bibliography of California Literature: Fiction of the Gold Rush Period, Drama of the Gold Rush*

Period, Poetry of the Gold Rush Period. New York: Burt Franklin, 1970.

J.S. Holliday, *The World Rushed In: The California Gold Rush Experience*. New York: Simon and Schuster, 1981.

Thomas Hunt, *Ghost Trails to California: A Pictorial Journey from the Rockies to the Gold Country*. Palo Alto, CA: American West, 1974.

Donald D. Jackson, *Gold Dust*. New York: Alfred A. Knopf, 1980.

Joseph H. Jackson, *Anybody's Gold: The Story of California's Mining Towns*. San Francisco: Chronicle Books, 1970.

George Keller, *A Trip Across the Plains and Life in California*. Oakland, CA: Biobooks, 1955.

Liza Ketchum, *The Gold Rush*. Boston: Little, Brown, 1996.

Leonard Kip, *California Sketches with Recollections of the Gold Mines*. Los Angeles: N.A. Kovach, 1946.

Jo Ann Levy, *They Saw the Elephant: Women in the California Gold Rush*. Hamden, CT: Archon Books, 1990.

William M'Ilvaine, *Sketches of Scenery and Notes of Personal Adventure in California*. San Francisco: Grabhorn Press, 1951.

Gwen Moffat, *Hard Road West: Alone on the California Trail*. New York: Viking, 1981.

Robert O'Brien, *California Called Them: A Saga of Golden Days and Roaring Camps*. New York: McGraw-Hill, 1951.

Brian Roberts, *American Alchemy: The California Gold Rush and Middle-Class Culture*. Chapel Hill: University of North Carolina Press, 2000.

Malcolm Rohrborough, *Days of Gold: The California Gold Rush and the American Nation*. Berkeley: University of California Press, 1997.

Andrew Rolle, *An American in California: The Biography of William Heath Davis, 1822–1909*. San Marino, CA: Huntington Library, 1956.

William Secrest, *Blood and Honor: Incredible, Yet Authentic Stories About the Wild Dueling Mania That Gripped California During the Gold Rush*. Fresno, CA: Saga-West, 1970.

Laurence Seidman, *The Fools of '49: The California Gold Rush, 1848–1856*. New York: Alfred A. Knopf, 1976.

Albert Shumate, *Boyhood Days: Ygnacio Villegas' Reminiscences of California in the 1850s*. San Francisco: California Historical Society, 1983.

Carl Wheat, *The Maps of the California Gold Region, 1848–1857: A Biblio-Cartography of an Important Decade*. San Francisco: Grabhorn Press, 1942.

Bob Young, *The Forty-Niners: The Story of the California Gold Rush*. New York: Julian Messner, 1966.

Periodicals

Henry Clay Bailey, "California '53: Journal of a California Pioneer," *Sutter County Historical Society News Bulletin*, April 1981.

Joan Barriaga, "Mary Bennett, the Black Knight's Lady," *The Californians*, September/October 1990.

Mary G. Bloom, ed., "The Hazelton Letters," *The Californians*, 1995.

Randy Brown, "Buried at Ash Hollow," *Overland Journal*, 1990.

Robert W. Carter, "'Sometimes When I Hear the Winds Sigh': Mortality on the Overland Trail," *California History*, Summer 1995.

William John Clarke, "Journey to the El Dorado: Diary of William John Clarke Jr.," *Wagon Wheels*, Fall 1986.

Hugh Davis, "Gold Rush Vignettes from Middlebourne: Letters of Anna E. Brown and Sibs," *Manuscripts*, 1982.

Alphonse A. Delepine, "'Among an Eminently Warlike People': Tales of a French Argonaut," *The Californians*, September/October 1988.

John Doble, "A Glimpse of Life in the Gold Country: Excerpts from John Doble's Journal and Correspondence," *California Geology*, 1994.

Patricia A. Etter, "To California on the Southern Route—1849," *Overland Journal*, Fall 1995.

Christiane Fischer, "Women in California in the Early 1850s," *Southern California Quarterly*, Fall 1978.

Joan C. Gorsuch, "Twice to the Mines: The Story of Addick Meentzen," *Chispa*, October–December 1975.

George Hoeper, "Stevenson's Regiment: Gold Rush Pioneers," *Las Calaveras*, April 1995.

D. Kaufman, "News from the Gold Fields," *Pacific Historian*, Fall 1976.

Stanislaus Lasselle, "The 1849 Diary of Stanislaus Lasselle," *Overland Journal*, 1991.

JoAnn Levy, "Crossing the Forty-Mile Desert: Sorrowful Recollections of Women Emigrants," *The Californians*, September/October 1987.

JoAnn Levy, "The Panama Trail: Short Cut to California," *Overland Journal*, Fall 1992.

Anne Lohrli, "'From California': Life in a Sierra Mining Camp, 1854," *Pacific Historian*, December 1980.

Carlos U. Lopez, "The Chilenos in the California Gold Rush," *The Californians*, March/April 1988.

Herbert C. Milikien, "'Dead of the Bloody Flux': Cholera Stalks the Emigrant Trail," *Overland Journal*, Autumn 1996.

Sandra L. Myres, "I Too Have Seen the Elephant: Women on the Overland Trails," *Overland Journal*, Fall 1986.

Irena P. Narell, "The Jewish '49er in the New Land of Milk and Honey," *The Californians*, March/April 1986.

Doyce B. Nunis, "Edward Gould Buffum: Early California Journalist," *California History*, Summer 1994.

Andrew J. Rotter, "'Matilda for God's Sake Write': Women and Families on the Argonaut Mind," *California History*, Summer 1979.

Lee A. Silva, "Snowshoe Thompson, America's Phenomenal Gold Rush Mailman," *The Californians*, November/December 1987.

Jack Smalley, "Gilded Luck," *Westways*, 1980.

R.M. Smith, "Source of Mother Lode Gold," *California Geology*, 1981.

Stan Steiner, "On the Trail of Joaquin Murieta," *American West*, January/February 1981.

Jan S. Stevens, "Stephen J. Field: A Gold Rush Lawyer Shapes the Nation," *Journal of the West*, July 1990.

Gerald Thompson, "Edward Fitzgerald Beale and the California Gold Rush, 1848–1850," *Southern California Quarterly*, Fall 1981.

Shih-Shan Henry Tsai, "The Chinese and 'Gold Mountain,'" *The Californians*, March/April 1988.

George T. Watkins, "Overland Travel, 1846–1853: A Trip Through a Junkyard Sewer," *Overland Journal*, Fall 1987.

Felix P. Wierzbicki, "California as It Is and as It May Be (1849), Part II: The Gold Region," *The Californians*, 1995.

Online Resources

Library of Congress, *California as I Saw It: First-Person Narratives of California's Early Years, 1849–1900.* Website located at http://memory.loc.gov/ammem/cbhtml/cbhome.html.

Index